MORE Wonderful Words

MIDDLE PRIMARY

herbivore devour swallow xylophone

ukelele

delicious embrace hues frock

by
Peter Clutterbuck

Viva Books

New Delhi | Mumbai | Chennai | Kolkata | Bangalore | Hyderabad

First Indian Edition 2007

VIVA BOOKS PRIVATE LIMITED

- 4737/23 Ansari Road, Daryaganj, New Delhi 110 002
  E-mail: vivadelhi@vivagroupindia.net, Tel. 42242200

- Plot No. 76, Service Industries, Shirvane, Sector 1, Nerul, Navi Mumbai 400 706
  E-mail: vivamumbai@vivagroupindia.net, Tel. 27721273, 27721274

- Jamals Fazal Chambers, 26 Greams Road, Chennai 600 006
  E-mail: vivachennai@vivagroupindia.net, Tel. 28290304, 28294241

- B-103, Jindal Towers, 21/1A/3 Darga Road, Kolkata 700 017
  E-mail: vivakolkata@vivagroupindia.net, Tel. 22836381, 22816713

- 7, Sovereign Park Apartments, 56-58, K. R. Road, Basavanagudi, Bangalore 560 004
  E-mail: vivabangalore@vivagroupindia.net, Tel.26607409, 26607410

- 101-102 Mughal Marc Apartments, 3-4-637 to 641, Narayanguda, Hyderabad 500 029
  E-mail: vivahyderabad@vivagroupindia.net, Tel. 27564481, 27564482

Published by arrangement with

Blake Publishing
655 Parramatta Road
Leichhardt NSW 2040
Australia

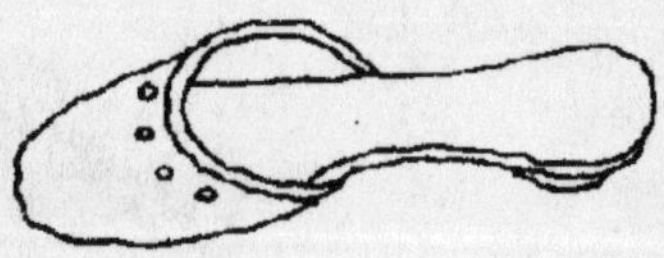

ISBN 81-309-0593-0

Published by Vinod Vasishtha for Viva Books Private Limited, 4737/23 Ansari Road
New Delhi-110 002. Printed and bound at Anand Sons, Delhi-110 092.

WONDERFUL WORDS – MIDDLE PRIMARY

This *Wonderful Words* book provides Middle Primary teachers with units of work aimed at building students' vocabulary and word knowledge.

The three books in this series aim to improve children's abilities to:
- increase vocabulary knowledge by looking at words around a theme
- define words and use a dictionary
- build word knowledge and recognise the parts of speech.

There are 36 double-page units – one for every week of the school year. Each 'A' unit has a theme heading, eg *In the Bathroom*. It begins with approximately thirty theme words that are grouped as parts of speech. These words can be used as a weekly spelling list and are used in a following exercise on Word Meanings.

Various activities then explore topics such as **Prefixes; Suffixes; Homographs; Homophones; Compound Words; Syllables; Anagrams; Synonyms; Antonyms; Classifications.** The A unit always ends with a short **Thinking** exercise.

On the left-hand page (the 'B' unit) there are one or two fun activities which can be worked individually or in pairs. These are based on discovering the magic of words and their meanings. The activities range from finding hidden words, word searches, classifying words and opposites to finding the odd one out, palindromes and word links.

These units help enhance student learning across the range of English outcomes. There are activities for all ability levels and students will look forward to learning through such diverse and enjoyable exercises.

Contents

Contents

UNIT 1A

In the Bathroom

▼ **Naming Words** *(Nouns)*	basin bath soap lather toothpaste shampoo mirror cabinet towel bathmat
● **Describing Words** *(Adjectives)*	frothy clean shiny slippery fresh damp spotless steamy dirty soapy
◆ **Action Words** *(Verbs)*	rinse brush bathe clean scrub relax spill squirt wipe wring

Write a story called "The Night I Was Sucked Down the Plughole." Use at least ten of the words above.

Word Meanings

Write the list words that have these meanings.

1 (▼) we clean our teeth with it ________

2 (▼) looking glass ________

3 (●) wet ________

4 (●) opposite of clean ________

5 (◆) rest ________

6 (◆) to rub hard ________

Dictionary – What's the Word?

Add the missing letters.

1 add _ _ _ _	*where you live*
2 adu _ _	*a grown up*
3 aero _ _ _ _ _ _	*flying machine*
4 alm _ _ _	*a type of nut*
5 alpha _ _ _ _	*letters of our language*

Word Endings – ary

Match each word in the box to its meaning.

library	*sanctuary*	*dictionary*
aviary	*canary*	*boundary*

1 a large bird cage ________

2 a small yellow bird ________

3 the edge of a sports ground ________

4 a place where wildlife is protected ________

5 a place where books can be borrowed ________

6 a book of word meanings ________

Special Words – Homophones

Choose a word from the box to fill the spaces below.

tail	*fare*	*hear*	*tale*	*fair*	*here*

1 The conductor took my bus ________.

2 The cat tried to bite its ________.

3 Would you ask Sally to come ________.

4 Our teacher told us a fairy ________.

5 My friend Sally has ________ coloured hair.

6 I could not ________ because of the noise.

Word Study – Word Groups

Colour the vegetable words red. Write the other words in the box under the correct heading below.

crimson	*gold*	*spinach*
carrot	*bicycle*	*tram*
hovercraft	*celery*	*purple*

Colour	Vehicle
________	________
________	________
________	________

Thinking

Make as many words as you can using these letters.

m t a e g

Gardening and School

UNIT 1B

A Eleven words in the grid relate to **gardening**. Colour them *green*.
Ten words in the grid relate to **school.** Colour them *blue*.

t	e	a	c	h	e	r	r	a	k	e	f
t	u	c	k	s	h	o	p	x	x	s	l
o	f	f	i	c	e	i	v	y	x	e	o
p	r	i	n	c	i	p	a	l	x	e	w
b	l	a	c	k	b	o	a	r	d	d	e
v	e	g	e	t	a	b	l	e	s	s	r
p	l	a	y	t	i	m	e	h	o	s	e
s	i	c	k	b	a	y	f	r	u	i	t
m	a	n	u	r	e	s	t	a	k	e	s
c	o	m	p	u	t	e	r	b	i	k	e
l	i	b	r	a	r	y	l	e	a	r	n
x	s	p	r	i	n	k	l	e	r	x	x

B

Flowers

Add the missing letters to the names of these flowers.

Draw a picture.

1 p__ns__ 2 __os__

3 __affo__ __ __ __ __ 4 __ai __ __

5 __arnat__ __ n 6 __opp__

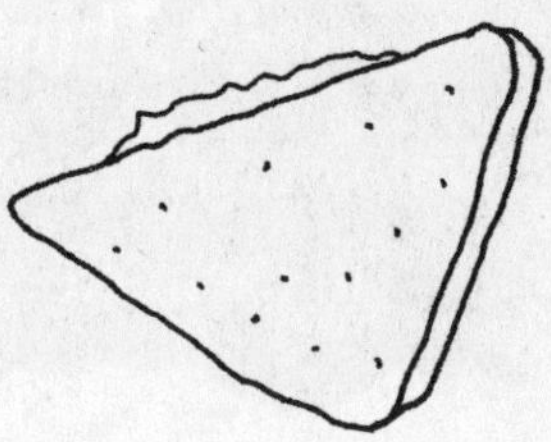

C

School

Write the names of eight things sold in your school tuckshop.

1 ______________________________

2 ______________________________

3 ______________________________

4 ______________________________

5 ______________________________

6 ______________________________

7 ______________________________

8 ______________________________

UNIT 2A

At the Beach

▼ **Naming Words** *(Nouns)*: sand towel waves shark pier umbrella jellyfish seaside seaweed sunscreen

● **Describing Words** *(Adjectives)*: calm sunny deep shallow wavy tanned sunburnt salty sandy choppy

◆ **Action Words** *(Verbs)*: sunbake paddle play swim splash explore build catch collect dive

Write a short story that begins "I was making a sandcastle when suddenly I saw something buried in the sand". Use some of the words above.

Word Meanings

Write the list words that have these meanings.

1 (▼) a cloth with which we dry ourselves ______

2 (▼) plants that grow in the ocean ______

3 (●) not deep ______

4 (●) brown skinned ______

5 (◆) to lie in the sun ______

6 (◆) to gather things ______

Dictionary – What's the Word?

Add the missing letters.

1 ans _ _ _ — *reply to a question*

2 aqu _ _ _ _ _ — *a place for fish*

3 asl _ _ _ — *not awake*

4 atl _ _ — *book of maps*

5 auth _ _ — *writer of stories*

6 aut _ _ _ — *a season of the year*

Word Beginnings – 'ex'

Match each word to its meaning.

1 no longer living	*excited*
2 to blow up like a bomb	*expand*
3 to grow larger	*extinct*
4 very happy and pleased	*extra*
5 very, very good	*explode*
6 something more	*excellent*

Special Words – Synonyms

In the grid find a word that has a similar meaning to each word below.

m	i	x	c	e	g
s	a	x	r	a	l
t	i	d	y	s	a
a	d	v	x	y	d
r	f	a	s	t	o
t	x	m	p	t	s

1 begin ______ 2 weep ______

3 help ______ 4 quick ______

5 simple ______ 6 happy ______

7 neat ______ 8 stir ______

Word Study – Matching Words

Match the words in the box to the words below.

whisker	*branch*	*book*
fish	*spider*	*flower*

1 tree ______ 2 index ______

3 petal ______ 4 web ______

5 gill ______ 6 cat ______

Thinking

Write down 10 words that have **oo** in them e.g. moon, poor.

Pairing Off

UNIT 2B

A Join the letter pairs correctly to make pairs of words belonging to a subject.

For example: ar pl pe um *two fruits* = pear plum

1	ue	pi	bl	nk	*two colours*	______	______
2	co	an	be	rn	*two vegetables*	______	______
3	kn	nd	ha	ee	*two body parts*	______	______
4	lt	up	so	sa	*two foods*	______	______
5	re	ma	at	go	*two farm animals*	______	______
6	pu	on	li	ma	*two large cats*	______	______
7	so	th	ba	ap	*two bathroom items*	______	______
8	tu	ca	rp	na	*two fish*	______	______
9	wk	ha	cr	ow	*two birds*	______	______
10	fl	th	mo	ea	*two insects*	______	______
11	nc	zi	ld	go	*two metals*	______	______
12	al	op	by	ru	*two gemstones*	______	______

B Add a pair of letters to complete each word so it matches the definition.
e.g. __ __ckey *sport:* Answer = hockey

1 __ __tter	*dairy food*	2 __ __ocolate	*sweet food*
3 __ __se	*flower*	4 __ __uare	*shape*
5 __ __ucer	*holds a cup*	6 __ __ctus	*prickly plant*
7 __ __ive	*oily fruit*	8 __ __brary	*place of books*
9 __ __rple	*colour*	10 __ __ffee	*hot drink*
11 __ __mond	*nut*	12 __ __ipper	*footwear*

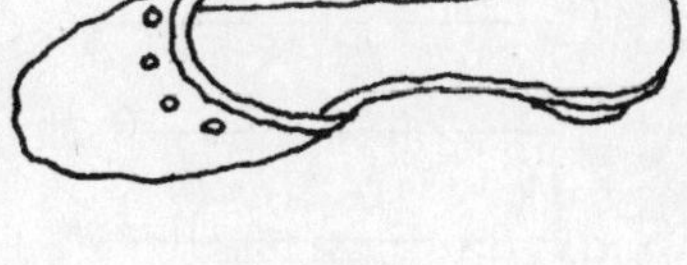

UNIT 3A

In the Classroom

▼ **Naming Words** *(Nouns)*	chalk teacher table desk television pencils pupils chalkboard notebooks keyboard
● **Describing Words** *(Adjectives)*	loud happy dull crowded busy lively untidy friendly bright active
◆ **Action Words** *(Verbs)*	answer copy help laugh learn understand work write talk listen

Write a story describing the best day you have ever had at school. Use at least 10 of the words above.

Word Meanings

Write the list words that have these meanings.

1 (▼) part of a computer ______________

2 (▼) a person who teaches ______________

3 (●) messy ______________

4 (●) noisy ______________

5 (◆) reply to a question ______________

6 (◆) to gain knowledge ______________

Dictionary – What's the Word?

Add the missing letters.

1 be _ _ _ _ *small insect*

2 bir _ _ _ _ _ *the day you were born*

3 blan _ _ _ *bed covering*

4 blizz _ _ _ *strong snow driven wind*

5 blo _ _ _ _ *flower on a tree*

6 bur _ _ _ _ *thief*

Word Endings – 'ent'

Match each word in the box to its meaning.

present	*parent*	*silent*
spent	*scent*	*present*

1 perfume ______________

2 noisy ______________

3 absent ______________

4 child ______________

5 money ______________

6 gift ______________

Special Words – Opposites

In the grid find a word that has an opposite meaning to each word below.

e	x	i	t	w	t	w
l	i	v	e	a	r	i
m	a	n	y	r	u	l
f	r	o	n	t	e	d
p	r	e	t	t	y	x

1 back ______________ 2 entrance ______________

3 tame ______________ 4 die ______________

5 false ______________ 6 peace ______________

7 few ______________ 8 ugly ______________

Word Study – Confused Words

Circle the correct word.

1 I *(saw, seen)* him yesterday.

2 The bird sang *(sweet, sweetly).*

3 He put *(his, he's)* rubbish in the bin.

4 The bottle is now *(vacant, empty).*

5 Mike decided to *(quite, quit)* his job.

6 He plays football *(good, well).*

Thinking

Write down ten words that have **ai** in them, e.g. train, brain.

Classifying

Find all the words in the grid. Write each under the correct heading below.

b	e	e	t	l	e	s	b	s	c
s	p	b	l	u	e	u	u	h	r
c	u	n	o	s	e	p	t	i	o
h	r	b	e	l	t	e	t	r	w
o	p	p	e	a	s	r	e	t	e
o	l	d	e	e	r	m	r	h	y
l	e	f	a	c	e	a	f	o	e
d	r	e	s	s	x	r	l	m	s
m	a	g	p	i	e	k	y	e	x
c	a	r	r	o	t	e	r	e	d
o	n	i	o	n	x	t	e	m	u
k	o	a	l	a	t	i	g	e	r

Clothing **Body Part** **Colour** **Insect**

Bird **Animal** **Vegetable** **Place**

UNIT 4A

Dinosaurs

▼ **Naming Words** *(Nouns)*	forest scales carnivore herbivore plants reptile Tyrannosaurus Rex Triceratops Stegosaurus Pterodactyl
● **Describing Words** *(Adjectives)*	cold-blooded deadly scaly scary massive gigantic horned ferocious huge tiny
◆ **Action Words** *(Verbs)*	growl grunt bite chew crunch stalk lurch lumber gash break

While walking in the bush you find a large egg. You take it home and put it under your bed. During the night you hear a noise coming from inside the egg. Write what happens.

Word Meanings

Write the list words that have these meanings.

1 (▼) a meat eater ____________

2 (▼) land covered with trees ____________

3 (●) very, very large ____________

4 (●) covered in scales ____________

5 (◆) make a noise like a pig ____________

6 (◆) grind up with the teeth ____________

Dictionary – What's the Word?

Add the missing letters.

1 cac _ _ _	*prickly plant*
2 can _ _ _	*small bird*
3 cap _ _ _ _	*leader of a team*
4 carn _ _ _ _ _ _	*flower*
5 cat _ _ _ _ _ _ _ _ _	*grub of a moth*
6 carr _ _ _ _	*part of a train*

Word Beginnings – 'de'

Match each word to its meaning.

1 to beat in a game	*dentist*
2 nice to taste	*decay*
3 policeman	*defeat*
4 person who cares for teeth	*detective*
5 to rot	*dessert*
6 part of a meal	*delicious*

Special Words – Compound Words

Join words in the box to make new words that match the pictures.
Write your answer underneath each picture.

arm	*door*	*chair*	*straw*
paper	*berry*	*news*	*bell*
brush	*sauce*	*tooth*	*pan*

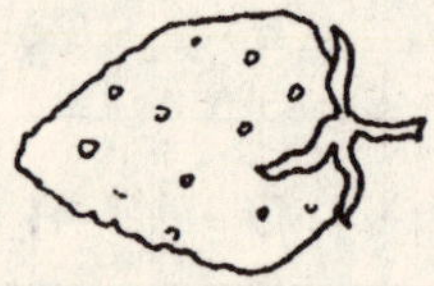

1 ____________

2 ____________

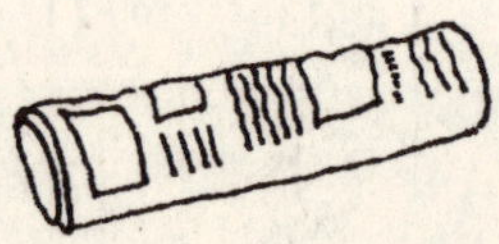

3 ____________

4 ____________

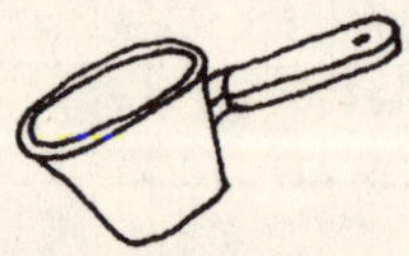

5 ____________

6 ____________

Word Study – Contractions

Write the two words that make up each contraction, e.g. it's = it is.

1 can't _____ _____ 2 he's _____ _____

3 we're _____ _____ 4 isn't _____ _____

5 they're _____ _____ 6 don't _____ _____

Jumbled Words

UNIT 4B

A Rearrange the letters to make a five-letter word to fit the definition, e.g. oersh *large animal* = horse.

1	alecm	*humped animal*	______	2	riach	*we sit on it*	______
3	nagit	*large person*	______	4	nifke	*it cuts*	______
5	enost	*rock*	______	6	wocrn	*a king wears one*	______
7	tsrfi	*opposite to last*	______	8	tsory	*tale*	______
9	rosht	*not tall*	______	10	daebr	*made from flour*	______
11	urtck	*large vehicle*	______	12	rboom	*we sweep with it*	______

B This time rearrange the letters to make six-letter words to match the definitions.

1	ytnetw	*number*	______	2	reddla	*climbing frame*	______
3	tibbra	*small animal*	______	4	enieng	*motor*	______
5	kcbuet	*water container*	______	6	cinpic	*outdoor lunch*	______
7	woholl	*not solid*	______	8	aswren	*opposite of question*	______
9	seeche	*dairy food*	______	10	elddsa	*seat on a horse*	______
11	elgjun	*dense forest*	______	12	ttkien	*baby cat*	______

C Unjumble the letters to make words to fit under the headings below.

udck	*lump*	*bare*	*museo*
tan	*leaf*	*low*	*pera*

Animal	**Fruit**	**Bird**	**Insect**
______	______	______	______
______	______	______	______

UNIT 5A

Magic

▼ **Naming Words** *(Nouns)*	fairy gnome goblin elf toadstool wizard witch wand ogre spell
● **Describing Words** *(Adjectives)*	beautiful amazing enchanting scary ugly magical spellbound wicked evil black
◆ **Action Words** *(Verbs)*	charm bewitch fly change vanish snatch soar rave creep glide

Imagine you have a magic wand that can turn things into anything you want. Make a list of things and what you would turn them into.

Word Meanings

Write the list words that have these meanings.

1 (▼) a fungus like a mushroom ____________

2 (▼) a male witch ____________

3 (●) unsightly to look at ____________

4 (●) astounding; incredible ____________

5 (◆) to disappear ____________

6 (◆) to grab quickly ____________

Dictionary – What's the Word?

Add the missing letters.

1 cen _ _ _ *the middle*

2 cen _ _ _ _ *a hundred years*

3 choc _ _ _ _ _ _ *sweet food*

4 corr _ _ _ _ _ _ _ *aboriginal ceremony*

5 crim _ _ _ *deep red colour*

6 curr _ _ _ *dried grape*

Word Endings – ure

Match each word in the box to its link word.

sure	*manure*	*cure*
future	*secure*	*furniture*

1 illness ________ 2 farmer ________

3 certain ________ 4 past ________

5 safe ________ 6 table ________

Special Words – Doubles

Match the doubles correctly.

go	*later*	*on*	*less*	*fro*	*by*

1 by and ________ 2 sooner or ________

3 touch and ________ 4 off and ________

5 to and ________ 6 more or ________

Word Study – Similies

Add a word from the box to complete the similies.

lightning	*ox*	*mouse*
coal	*bee*	

1 as strong as an ____________

2 as quick as ____________

3 as quiet as a ____________

4 as busy as a ____________

5 as black as ____________

Word Study – Collections

Use a word from the box to fill the spaces.

bunch	*box*	*string*	*batch*	*clutch*	*herd*

1 a ________ of pearls 2 a ________ of matches

3 a ________ of grapes 4 a ________ of cattle

5 a ________ of eggs 6 a ________ of bread

Thinking

Find and write all the smaller words inside these words.

1 refreshment 2 therein 3 newspaper

Small Words

UNIT 5B

A Look at each word carefully. Find and write a smaller word that matches the definition beside it, e.g. elephant *insect* = ant.

1 attendance	*number*	________	**2** apricot	*baby's bed*	________
3 licorice	*cereal*	________	**4** allowed	*not high*	________
5 despondent	*small pool*	________	**6** scowl	*bird*	________
7 crockery	*large stone*	________	**8** advantage	*insect*	________
9 caterpillar	*tablet*	________	**10** address	*clothing*	________
11 board	*paddle*	________	**12** infantry	*baby*	________

B Now do the same for these.

1 intention	*canvas home*	________	**2** saucer	*added to pie*	________
3 imposter	*part of fence*	________	**4** stealthily	*take*	________
5 hypotenuse	*cooking item*	________	**6** shopping	*jump on one leg*	________
7 slaughter	*to giggle*	________	**8** shampoo	*meat of a pig*	________
9 sparrow	*bow and*	________	**10** scream	*dairy food*	________
11 stupendous	*writing instrument*	______	**12** transparent	*mother or father*	______

C Add the small words in the box to the spaces below to complete the names of animals and birds.

or	*rich*	*pie*
ark	*as*	*ant*

1 h ______ se	*riding animal*	**2** mag ______	*black and white bird*
3 w ______ p	*stinging insect*	**4** ost ______	*very, very large bird*
5 sh ______	*large fish*	**6** eleph ______	*large animal with a trunk*

In the Forest

▼	**Naming Words** *(Nouns)*	branch jungle trees canopy bush scrub trunk thicket sapling foliage
●	**Describing Words** *(Adjectives)*	bushy scary evergreen leafy gigantic hardy thick mossy prickly woody
◆	**Action Words** *(Verbs)*	chop die saw sprout wind buzz rustle grow crack cut

Make a list of creatures that live on or near a tree.
Draw some pictures.

Word Meanings

Write the list words that have these meanings.

1 (▼) dense forest ____________

2 (▼) the leaves of a tree ____________

3 (●) very, very large ____________

4 (●) covered in spines or thorns ____________

5 (◆) the noise of a bee ____________

6 (◆) to grow into life as a seed does ____________

Dictionary – What's the Word?

Add the missing letters.

1 dec _ _ _	*period of ten years*
2 det _ _ _ _ _ _ _	*policeman*
3 dia _ _ _ _	*precious stone*
4 dic _ _ _ _ _ _ _ _ _	*book of word meanings*
5 din _ _	*native dog*
6 din _ _ _ _ _ _	*extinct reptile*

Word Beginnings – 'con'

Match each word to its meaning.

1 musical items performed	*confetti*
2 paper thrown at a wedding	*concert*
3 a prisoner	*contest*
4 a large land mass	*convict*
5 people in a church	*continent*
6 a competition or race	*congregation*

Special Words – Homophones

Find a word in the grid that sounds the same but has a different spelling and a different meaning to a word in the box. On a separate sheet of paper write the words in sentences to show you know their meanings.

tow dear blue whole hour fur

h	o	l	e	o	u	r
t	o	e	b	l	e	w
d	e	e	r	f	i	r

1 tow – toe

2 ____________

3 ____________

4 ____________

5 ____________

6 ____________

Word Study – Word Groups

Circle the word that does not belong in each group.

1	red	yellow	purple	bus
2	peach	carrot	plum	apple
3	celery	sparrow	wren	magpie
4	horse	bear	tiger	lizard
5	bee	spider	ant	butterfly
6	sun	moon	stars	ocean

Making Words

Use the letters of the words in capital letters to write words that fit the definitions. The first letters have been given to help you.

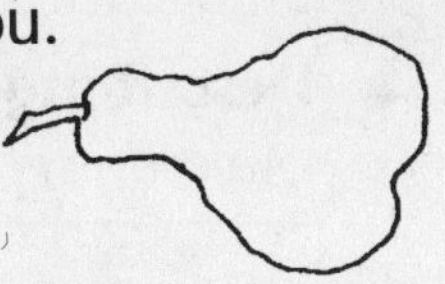

A

PERSONALITY

1 *very, very small* t ________	2 *fruit* p ________
3 *small horse* p ________	4 *what a thief does* s ________
5 *small rock* s ________	6 *old, not fresh* s ________
7 *your backbone* s ________	8 *you use it to breathe* n ________

B

LEPRECHAUNS

1 *frighten* s ________	2 *not expensive* c ________
3 *skin of an orange* p ________	4 *to arrive* r ________
5 *fruit* p ________	6 *a fold in paper* c ________
7 *hospital worker* n ________	8 *opposite to there* h ________
9 *dried plum* p ________	10 *to go after* c ________
11 *hard hit to face* s ________	12 *to jump in the air* l ________

C

ARCHAEOLOGIST

1 *you score a* g ________ *in football*	2 *riding animal* h ________
3 *farmyard bird* g ________	4 *grain store* s ________
5 *not all* s ________	6 *footwear* s ________
7 *not tight* l ________	8 *place to buy goods* s ________

9 *it pumps blood around the body* h ________

10 *scary, it haunts old places* g ________

UNIT 7A

Football

▼ **Naming Words** *(Nouns)* — goals boots boundary oval umpire jumpers socks kick whistle crowd

● **Describing Words** *(Adjectives)* — fast dirty muddy tired tough quick injured powerful long sore

◆ **Action Words** *(Verbs)* — kick bounce dodge chase mark tackle score dash fumble pass

Which is the better game, football or cricket?
Write a paragraph giving your opinion.

Word Meanings

Write the list words that have these meanings.

1 (▼) place where games are played ____________

2 (▼) person who sees the rules are obeyed ____________

3 (●) unclean ____________

4 (●) hurt ____________

5 (◆) to run after ____________

Dictionary – What's the Word?

Add the missing letters.

1 ea _ _ _ — *large bird of prey*

2 e _ _ — *a large bird*

3 ent _ _ _ _ _ — *opposite to exit*

4 eucal _ _ _ _ _ — *a gum tree*

5 exp _ _ _ _ _ _ — *very dear to buy*

Word Endings – 'et'

Match each word in the box to its meaning.

violet	*crumpet*	*planet*
bonnet	*trumpet*	*basket*

1 a musical instrument ____________

2 a toasted food ____________

3 a body that orbits the Sun ____________

4 a container ____________

5 a flower ____________

6 a head covering ____________

Special Words – Synonyms

Unjumble the letters in brackets to make a word that means the same as the underlined word.

1 At the zoo we saw a <u>donkey</u>. *(sas)* ________

2 She got the <u>correct</u> answer. *(ghtri)* ________

3 Mike tried to <u>frighten</u> me. *(secar)* ________

4 Mr Jones is aged. *(ldo)* ________

5 What is the <u>cost</u> of butter? *(rpice)* ________

6 We are <u>nearly</u> there. *(lamsto)* ________

Word Study – Receptacles

Match each word in the box to one below.

water	*coins*	*flowers*
food	*cups*	*letter*

1 vase ________ 2 kettle ________

3 cupboard ________ 4 purse ________

5 envelope ________ 6 hamper ________

Thinking

Make two words from each group of letters.

1 acer 2 drea

3 flwo 4 ilve

5 plma 6 mtae

Dictionary Dazzlers

UNIT 7B

It is important that you know how to use a dictionary to check word spellings and meanings. Use your dictionary while you work on these exercises.

A Add the missing letters to these words.

1	det _ _ _ _ _ _ _ _	*policeman*	2	el _ _ _ _ _ _ _ _	*large animal*
3	sk _ _ _	*smelly animal*	4	la _ _	*baby sheep*
5	ho _ _ _ _ _ _	*day off work*	6	fo _ _ _ _ _	*thick bush*
7	si _ _ _ _	*precious metal*	8	mo _ _ _ _ _ _ _ _	*very high hill*
9	ye _ _ _ _ _	*colour*	10	ca _ _ _ _ _ _	*leader of a team*
11	spa _ _ _ _ _ _ _ _	*pasta*	12	bo _ _ _ _ _	*container for liquid*

B Now do the same for these.

1	_ _ _ ine	*motor*	2	_ _ own	*a king wears one*
3	_ _ _ gle	*thick forest*	4	_ _ _ tle	*reptile with shell*
5	_ _ gar	*sweetener*	6	_ _ _ mer	*hot season*
7	_ _ tten	*baby cat*	8	_ _ _ bit	*small, furry animal*
9	_ _ _ ning	*opposite to afternoon*	10	_ _ _ ger	*part of your hand*
11	_ _ _ ber	*wood for building*	12	_ _ uck	*large vehicle*

C Colour the correct box.

	Yes	No
1 A **farrier** is a person who shoes horses.		
2 **Crimson** is a dark green colour.		
3 **Mutton** is the meat of a cow.		
4 Another name for sauce is **ketchup.**		
5 A **piranha** is a type of fish.		
6 A **llama** is a type of fruit.		
7 A **ruby** is a red-coloured stone.		
8 A **lynx** is a type of cat.		

UNIT 8A

In the Garden

▼	**Naming Words** *(Nouns)*	flowers rake manure stakes compost shrubs shovel spade hoe scarecrow
●	**Describing Words** *(Adjectives)*	blooming beautiful flowery grassy leafy weedy dry shady frosty neat
◆	**Action Words** *(Verbs)*	dig burn germinate mow pollinate spray water weed trim mulch

Make a list of vegetable and flower words. Draw pictures of them.

Word Meanings

Write the list words that have these meanings.

1 (▼) a digging tool ______________

2 (▼) small trees ______________

3 (●) nice to look at ______________

4 (●) full of weeds ______________

5 (◆) to grow as seeds do ______________

6 (◆) to destroy with fire ______________

Dictionary – What's the Word?

Add the missing letters.

1	fac _ _ _ _	*place where things are made*
2	fa _ _	*a baby deer*
3	fi _ _ _ _	*a violin*
4	flam _ _ _ _	*large water bird*
5	flo _ _ _ _	*person who sells flowers*
6	fou _ _ _ _ _	*a water spout*

Word Beginnings – 'in'

Match each word in the box to its meaning.

insects	*infant*	*insane*
invisible	*invent*	*ink*

1 not able to be seen ______________

2 writing fluid ______________

3 to make something new ______________

4 a baby ______________

5 small, six-legged creatures ______________

6 mad ______________

Special Words – Opposites

Replace each of the underlined words with its opposite from the box.

kind	*fat*	*sharp*
below	*dead*	*shallow*

1 This old knife is blunt. ______________

2 Those pigs are quite thin. ______________

3 She is cruel to the puppies. ______________

4 The old tree is alive. ______________

5 This end of the pool is deep. ______________

6 The shelf is above the sink. ______________

Word Study – Syllables

Join the syllables to make a word,
e.g. (mum i max) = *maximum*

1 (ful beau ti) ______________

2 (dan ous ger) ______________

3 (ex ment cite) ______________

4 (clud con ed) ______________

5 (en cal dar) ______________

6 (i day hol) ______________

Thinking

Make two words from each group of letters.

1 lpae	2 gnir
3 desi	4 onw
5 mnae	6 srohe

Fish and Trees

A Ten words in the grid are related to **fish**. Colour them *red*.
Ten words in the grid are related to **trees**. Colour them *green*.

s	b	l	f	i	n	s	r	o	o	t	s
c	r	e	s	p	i	n	n	e	r	n	s
a	a	a	f	i	l	l	e	t	x	e	o
l	n	v	o	c	t	o	p	u	s	s	i
e	c	e	h	o	l	l	o	w	s	t	l
s	h	s	t	r	u	n	k	l	i	n	e
f	l	i	p	p	e	r	s	p	a	w	n
c	a	n	o	p	y	x	x	b	a	r	k
e	u	c	a	l	y	p	t	u	s	x	x
h	o	o	k	s	i	n	k	e	r	x	x

B One very large fish is the shark. The word *shark* contains the **ar** letter pattern. Add **ar** or **or** to these words.

1 t_____ch **2** p_____k **3** sh_____e

4 g_____den **5** sn_____e **6** t_____get

C Label all the parts of this tree.

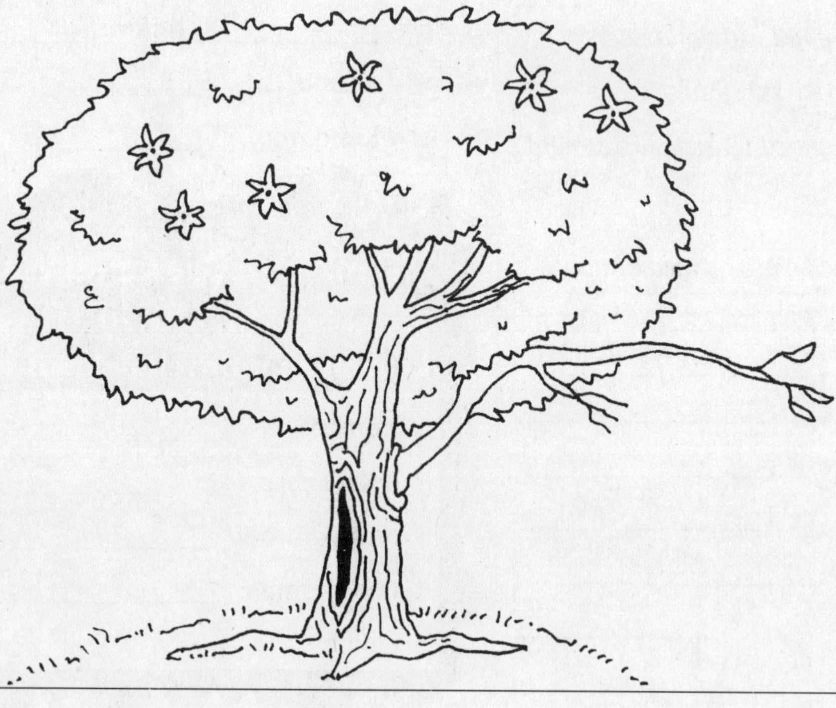

trunk
roots
branch
leaves
twig
hollow
bark
blossom

UNIT 9A

Haunted Houses

▼ **Naming Words** *(Nouns)*	ghost mystery demon castle witch spirit terror vampire midnight ghouls
● **Describing Words** *(Adjectives)*	eerie secret secluded dangerous ghostly pale moonlit weird spooky
◆ **Action Words** *(Verbs)*	clank hoot scream screech tremble whisper seize shriek frighten shiver

Imagine you are a ghost. Write down some mischievous things you would do to scare your friends.

Word Meanings

Write the list words that have these meanings.

1 (▼) strange happening ______

2 (▼) great fear ______

3 (●) strange, odd ______

4 (●) unsafe ______

5 (◆) shake with fear ______

6 (◆) to yell loudly ______

Dictionary – What's the Word?

Add the missing letters.

1 gall _ _ — *the movement of a horse*

2 gar _ _ _ — *place where flowers grow*

3 ge _ _ _ — *farm birds*

4 gir _ _ _ _ — *animal with long neck*

5 gl _ _ — *sticky substance*

6 gui _ _ _ — *stringed musical instrument*

Word Endings – 'er'

Match each word in the box to its meaning.

feathers	*quarter*	*leather*
setter	*plover*	*wander*

1 a kind of bird ______

2 a kind of dog ______

3 roam ______

4 hide of cattle ______

5 one fourth ______

6 covering of a bird ______

Special Words – Compounds

Join two words in the box to make a compound word. Write them in the spaces below.

stick	*space*	*paste*	*water*
shoe	*horse*	*mill*	*wind*
ship	*tooth*	*fall*	*lip*

1 ______ 2 ______

3 ______ 4 ______

5 ______ 6 ______

Word Study – Australian Words

Match each Australian word to its meaning.

bellyflop	*gum*	*galah*
joey	*station*	*koala*

1 bird ______ 2 tree ______

3 dive ______ 4 farm ______

6 furry animal ______

6 baby kangaroo ______

Thinking - Cramped Words

Find a word to match the meanings.

kennelephantinyellowlambeanine

1 number ______

2 baby sheep ______

3 large animal ______

4 dogs home ______

5 colour ______

Sounds Like

Words do not have to look the same to have a similar sound.

A Write a word from the box beside the word it rhymes with.

score	*farm*	*does*	*steers*	*paw*	*core*
brought	*male*	*tight*	*care*	*feet*	*killed*

1 *straw* rhymes with ______________

2 *buzz* rhymes with ______________

3 *palm* rhymes with ______________

4 *write* rhymes with ______________

5 *trail* rhymes with ______________

6 *four* rhymes with ______________

7 *stair* rhymes with ______________

8 *tears* rhymes with ______________

9 *seat* rhymes with ______________

10 *caught* rhymes with ______________

11 *build* rhymes with ______________

12 *poor* rhymes with ______________

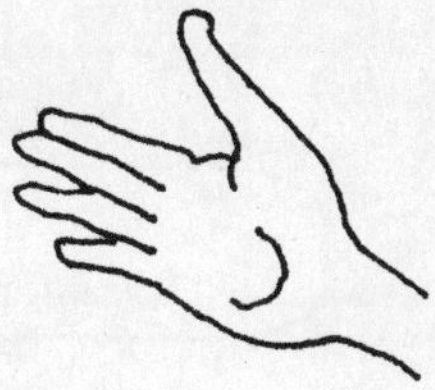

B Add the word that sounds like the underlined word but has the meaning given.

1 Sounds like <u>fold</u> and means *a precious metal.* ______________

2 Sounds like <u>house</u> and means *a small animal.* ______________

3 Sounds like <u>sheep</u> and means *a quick look.* ______________

4 Sounds like <u>heard</u> and means *a creature that flies.* ______________

5 Sounds like <u>water</u> and means *a female child.* ______________

6 Sounds like <u>deer</u> and means *twelve months.* ______________

7 Sounds like <u>cream</u> and means *a small river.* ______________

8 Sounds like <u>red</u> and means *a food made from flour.* ______________

9 Sounds like <u>shoe</u> and means *a colour.* ______________

10 Sounds like <u>firm</u> and means *a creature that burrows in the earth.* ______________

11 Sounds like <u>were</u> and means *the covering of a bear.* ______________

12 Sounds like <u>shell</u> and means *something that rings.* ______________

UNIT 10A

Horses

▼	**Naming Words** *(Nouns)*	saddle pony bridle halter hoof gelding mare blacksmith filly stable
●	**Describing Words** *(Adjectives)*	chestnut frisky piebald hoofed roan mounted swift champion lame tame
◆	**Action Words** *(Verbs)*	bolt gallop trot rear race mount kick ride stomp pig-root

Write a fact sheet on horses. List at least 5 facts.
e.g. A male horse is a stallion. Draw some pictures.

Word Meanings

Write the list words that have these meanings.

1 (▼) a small horse ____________________

2 (▼) riding seat on a horse ____________________

3 (●) black and white ____________________

4 (●) to be sore in a leg ____________________

5 (◆) to get on a horse's back ____________________

6 (◆) to move as a racehorse does ____________________

Dictionary – What's the Word?

Add the missing letters.

1 ha _ _	*covering of the head*
2 har _ _ _ _	*spear*
3 heli _ _ _ _ _ _ _	*flying machine*
4 herr _ _ _	*small fish*
5 hex _ _ _ _	*six-sided figure*
6 hos _ _ _ _ _	*place for sick people*

Word Beginnings – 'pre'

Match each word to its meaning.

1 a gift	*precious*
2 to push with a finger	*prepare*
3 very valuable	*present*
4 nice to look at	*press*
5 the animal being hunted	*pretty*
6 to get things ready	*prey*

Special Words – Doubles

Add a word from the box to complete these doubles.

again	*downs*	*chairs*
fast	*sauce*	*take*

1 We stacked the tables and __________ in the room.

2 You have to learn to give and __________.

3 I have told you again and __________ not to do it.

4 He has had a lot of ups and __________ lately.

5 She ate a pie with __________.

6 It is a hard and __________ rule at our school.

Word Study – Slang Words

Match each slang word to its meaning below.

baabaa	*fangs*	*bomb*
tenner	*mutt*	*cool*

1 old car ____________________

2 teeth ____________________

3 sheep ____________________

4 very good ____________________

5 dog ____________________

6 ten dollars ____________________

Thinking

Make a list of words that name parts of a tree

Word Links

UNIT 10B

We can link words in different ways.

For example, **hot** and **cold** can be linked because they are opposites.
Horse and **saddle** can be linked because we use a saddle when we ride a horse.

A Write the words in the box beside the words that they can be linked with.

lightening	*beach*	*hand*	*carrot*
heart	*knee*	*glass*	*branch*
square	*chips*	*bow*	*nurse*

1 arrow ____________ 2 potato ____________
3 finger ____________ 4 hospital ____________
5 leg ____________ 6 thunder ____________
7 vegetable ____________ 8 circle ____________
9 bottle ____________ 10 sandcastle ____________
11 kidney ____________ 12 tree ____________

B Find words in the grid and write them beside their link words on the right.

f	o	a	l	w	s	y
b	b	s	m	o	t	e
a	a	h	l	o	a	a
l	t	u	l	l	r	r
l	h	t	k	s	t	c
b	i	r	d	t	w	u
n	o	s	e	y	o	p

1 soap ____________
2 sheep ____________
3 open ____________
4 moon ____________
5 fire ____________
6 month ____________
7 bat ____________
8 nest ____________
9 horse ____________
10 pig ____________
11 three ____________
12 saucer ____________
13 smell ____________

UNIT 11A

In the Jungle

▼ **Naming Words** *(Nouns)*	creepers canopy ferns vines rainforest downpour fronds shade cloudburst animal
● **Describing Words** *(Adjectives)*	hidden steamy shrubby dense tropical mossy moist misty tangled dark
◆ **Action Words** *(Verbs)*	climb compete drip strangle swing pour smother grow cover dwell

Write a story called "Lost in the Jungle." Use at least ten of the words above.

Word Meanings

Write the list words that have these meanings.

1 (▼) the top of a rainforest ______

2 (▼) a sudden falling of heavy rain ______

3 (●) very thick ______

4 (●) wet, damp ______

5 (◆) to choke ______

6 (◆) to live somewhere ______

Dictionary – What's the Word?

Add the missing letters.

1 ide _ _ _ _ _ _ _ _ *exactly the same*

2 imp _ _ _ _ _ _ *rude*

3 in _ _ _ _ _ _ *small insects*

4 in _ _ _ _ *opposite to outside*

5 inv _ _ _ *to make something new*

6 is _ _ _ _ *land surrounded by water*

Word Endings – 'el'

Match each word in the box to its meaning.

cruel	*quarrel*	*jewel*
motel	*camel*	*angel*

1 precious stone ______

2 argument ______

3 animal with a hump ______

4 heavenly person ______

5 unkind ______

6 a place to stay ______

Special Words – Anagrams

Rearrange the letters of the words in the box to make a word that matches the definition.

lump	*save*	*pale*	*seat*	*time*	*diet*

1 a fruit ______

2 container for flowers ______

3 to jump in the air ______

4 direction ______

5 small insect ______

6 rise and fall of the ocean ______

Word Study – Places

Match each place to a link word below.

theatre	*quarry*	*garage*
aquarium	*aviary*	

1 stone ______ 2 car ______

3 movie ______ 4 birds ______

5 fish ______

Thinking

These words have been cramped.
Find a word to match the meaning.

yachtentadpolettuce

1 boat with sails ______

2 green vegetable ______

3 number ______

4 canvas home ______

5 baby frog ______

Out of Place Words

UNIT 11B

In each group colour the word that does not belong.
e.g. cat dog horse eagle lion — **eagle** is out of place because it is a bird.

A

1	sparrow	wren	magpie	emu	cat
2	root	pencil	branch	twig	leaf
3	duck	lion	elephant	horse	donkey
4	apple	peach	carrot	pear	grape
5	bottle	beans	peas	potatoes	turnips
6	comet	star	planet	satellite	freeway
7	uncle	aunt	sister	fence	brother
8	rose	kettle	daffodil	daisy	pansy
9	wheel	tyre	brakes	pedals	petrol
10	thousand	century	million	school	dozen
11	decade	month	towel	year	week
12	geranium	knife	fork	spoon	chopsticks

You might find these a little harder.
e.g. window bottle mirror knife tumbler — **knife** is out of place because it is made of steel but the others can all be made of glass.

B

1	penguin	skunk	magpie	zebra	donkey
2	apple	peach	almond	pear	nectarine
3	honey	milk	cheese	yoghurt	cream
4	nephew	mother	father	brother	boy
5	magpie	pigeon	bat	eagle	hawk
6	trumpet	bugle	violin	recorder	flute
7	milk	wood	oil	water	petrol
8	ankle	toe	foot	shin	eye
9	ruby	emerald	sapphire	iron	diamond
10	apples	peanuts	potatoes	carrots	onions
11	bacon	mutton	cheese	pork	steak
12	crocodile	fish	alligator	lizard	platypus

UNIT 12A

Monsters

▼ **Naming Words** *(Nouns)* — demon dragon giant vampire zombie bunyip bogeyman mammoth satyr voodoo

● **Describing Words** *(Adjectives)* — vicious angry gigantic enormous dangerous cursed terrifying scary wicked wild

◆ **Action Words** *(Verbs)* — capture clasp harm snatch suck devour pounce maul bound seize

Draw a monster. Give it a name.
Describe where it came from and what it does.

Word Meanings

Write the list words that have these meanings.

1 (▼) a large extinct animal like an elephant ____________

2 (▼) a creature that sucks blood ____________

3 (●) evil ____________

4 (●) very savage ____________

5 (◆) to eat, consume ____________

6 (◆) to grab and hold ____________

Dictionary – What's the Word?

Add the missing letters.

1 jag _ _ _ *large cat*

2 Jan _ _ _ _ *month of the year*

3 je _ _ _ *sweet food*

4 jew _ _ _ *precious stones*

5 ju _ _ _ *the liquid of fruit*

6 ju _ _ _ _ *very thick forest*

Word Beginnings – 'pro'

Match each word to its meaning.

1 a teacher at a university	*procession*
2 to care for someone	*propeller*
3 a parade	*protect*
4 to poke	*prod*
5 part of a plane	*professor*
6 a wise saying	*proverb*

Special Words – Homophones

Circle the correct word in the brackets.

1 I picked a sweet smelling (*rose rows*).

2 Yesterday I had a (*hair hare*) cut.

3 This meat is still (*roar raw*).

4 The (*hair hare*) ran quickly when it heard the dogs bark.

5 I could hear the (*roar raw*) of the lion.

6 The glasses were placed in neat (*rose rows*).

Word Study – Word Groups

Add a word from the box to complete each row.

rose	*seat*	*bus*
bark	*cheese*	*banjo*

1 truck, car, taxi ____________

2 violin, guitar, piano ____________

3 chair, table, stool ____________

4 milk, yoghurt, cream ____________

5 daffodil, pansy, daisy ____________

6 trunk, limb, branch ____________

Thinking

Make a list of words that name things you could find inside your refrigerator.

Hide and Seek

UNIT 12B

A In each sentence a word has been hidden. It may form part of a longer word or be part of two or more words.
For example: A re**d og**re was seen in the yard. *(animal)* Answer = dog

Find each hidden word that matches the definition.

1 Her head rumbled loudly. *(musical instrument)* ____________

2 He likes to sing love songs. *(worn on the hand)* ____________

3 The board was smothered in paint. *(parent)* ____________

4 Get my cap, please. *(fruit)* ____________

5 This gizmo uses lots of fuel. *(small animal)* ____________

6 They did the skit ten times. *(baby animal)* ____________

7 We decided to clap each time he sang. *(fruit)* ____________

8 After the dive you must reach air quickly. *(we sit on it)* ____________

9 The padre ambled across the field. *(you do it when asleep)* ____________

10 I am glad derelicts are not allowed. *(climbing frame)* ____________

11 Price real roses please. *(breakfast food)* ____________

12 It doesn't take much to astonish him. *(cooked bread)* ____________

B In 1 - 6 find the hidden animals. In 7 - 12 find the hidden birds.

1 He came late. ____________

2 I saw the fair at noon. ____________

3 Leap every day. ____________

4 He will be a rover. ____________

5 I gave Don keys to the house. ____________

6 Do go to the zoo. ____________

7 Don't grasp arrows. ____________

8 Put the hem up. ____________

9 Don't rob inside the house. ____________

10 Try not to scowl. ____________

11 We saw lots of beagles. ____________

12 There is a large crowd there. ____________

UNIT 13A

Families

▼ **Naming Words** *(Nouns)*: brother sister niece nephew uncle aunt sibling parent love home

● **Describing Words** *(Adjectives)*: loyal loving caring sharing elder helpful fun-loving spiteful kind

◆ **Action Words** *(Verbs)*: play help hinder fight squabble show share speak chatter laugh

Make a fact sheet on your family. Write at least five facts.
e.g. I have a younger sister called Jessie.

Word Meanings

Write the list words that have these meanings.

1 (▼) your father's sister ____________

2 (▼) where a family lives ____________

3 (●) generous ____________

4 (●) worries about others ____________

5 (◆) to argue loudly ____________

6 (◆) to talk quickly ____________

Dictionary – What's the Word?

Add the missing letters.

1 kan _ _ _ _ _ *hopping animal*

2 ken _ _ _ *dog's home*

3 ket _ _ _ *we boil water in it*

4 kil _ _ _ _ _ *a weight of 1 000 grams*

5 ki _ _ _ _ *baby cat*

6 kn _ _ _ _ _ *joint of the finger*

Word Endings – 'ble'

Match each word in the box to its meaning.

grumble	*double*	*stable*
stumble	*possible*	*marble*

1 to trip ____________

2 able to be done ____________

3 hard rock ____________

4 twice ____________

5 horse's home ____________

6 complain ____________

Special Words – Synonyms

Choose a word from the box to replace the underlined word.

obtain	*ache*	*fast*
lead	*rich*	*gem*

1 This toy car is very quick. ____________

2 She had a pain in her arm. ____________

3 He tried to get a new address. ____________

4 The precious jewel was stolen. ____________

5 Mr Smith is very wealthy. ____________

6 She will guide us to the caves. ____________

Word Study – Matching Words

Match the words in the box to the words below.

reservoir	*bed*	*hammer*
headlines	*head*	

1 newspaper ____________

2 mattress ____________

3 bonnet ____________

4 nail ____________

5 water ____________

Thinking

Make a list of words that name things you could find in a bathroom.

Trains and Reptiles

UNIT 13B

A Ten words in the grid relate to **trains.** Colour them *black.*
Ten words in the grid relate to **reptiles.** Colour them *green.*

s	t	a	t	i	o	n	r	w	h	t	c
p	s	c	a	l	e	s	a	h	i	i	o
l	p	o	i	s	o	n	i	e	b	m	n
a	l	i	z	a	r	d	l	e	e	e	d
t	f	a	n	g	s	x	s	l	r	t	u
f	g	u	a	r	d	x	p	s	n	a	c
o	t	i	c	k	e	t	r	s	a	b	t
r	g	e	c	k	o	x	e	e	t	l	o
m	v	e	n	o	m	x	y	a	e	e	r
c	a	r	r	i	a	g	e	t	x	x	x
c	r	o	c	o	d	i	l	e	x	x	x
c	o	l	d	b	l	o	o	d	e	d	x

B The word *trains* contains the **ai** letter pattern. Add the ai pattern to each space and draw a picture of the word you make.

1 h____r

2 p____nt

3 ch____r

4 d____sy

5 ch____n

6 sn____l

Parties

▼ **Naming Words** *(Nouns)*	birthday present cakes balloons barbeque lollies streamers cordial jelly pastries
● **Describing Words** *(Adjectives)*	busy happy exciting jolly merry welcoming friendly delicious charming trendy
◆ **Action Words** *(Verbs)*	drink eat embrace guzzle sing toast feast enjoy laugh congratulate

Make a list of all the foods and drinks you would like to have at your next party.

Word Meanings

Write the list words that have these meanings.

1 (▼) cooking meat outside ______________

2 (▼) a celebration of the date of your birth ______________

3 (●) tasting good ______________

4 (●) always doing things ______________

5 (◆) hug ______________

6 (◆) to drink quickly ______________

Dictionary – What's the Word?

Add the missing letters.

1 la _ _ _ _ *climbing frame*

2 la _ _ *baby sheep*

3 lau _ _ _ _ *place to wash clothes*

4 lea _ _ _ _ *what shoes are often made of*

5 leo _ _ _ _ *spotted, large cat*

6 lett _ _ _ *leafy, green vegetable*

Word Beginnings – 'sur'

Match each word to its meaning.

1 to give in	*surface*
2 to be certain	*surf*
3 a doctor who operates	*surname*
4 your family name	*surgeon*
5 the ocean waves	*sure*
6 the top layer	*surrender*

Special Words – Opposites

Write words with opposite meanings.
The word you write must have 4 letters.

1 none ________	2 less ________
3 strong ________	4 whisper ________
5 win ________	6 entrance ________
7 foolish ________	8 work ________

Word Study – Confused Words

Underline the correct word.

1 The bird *(lay laid)* the egg yesterday.

2 They *(were where)* playing in the yard.

3 I finally *(chose choosed)* my present.

4 *(There They're)* waiting for us to arrive.

5 The dog *(who that)* bit him is here.

6 He fell *(of off)* the bridge.

Thinking

Join the groups of letters to make two words in each line.

1 fa/be/rm/ll ________ ________

2 ba/fl/ag/by ________ ________

3 st/we/ar/ek ________ ________

4 sh/gr/ow/ot ________ ________

5 le/ft/ca/rd ________ ________

6 ye/wa/ar/sh ________ ________

Cramped Words

UNIT 14B

A These words have been written without spaces.

lambknifewolfshoenorthmicesevenquickblueflytoerose

Find and write the word to match each definition.

1 insect ____________
2 fast ____________
3 animals that eat cheese ____________
4 footwear ____________
5 cutting implement ____________
6 baby sheep ____________
7 large dog ____________
8 a flower ____________
9 part of the foot ____________
10 a number ____________
11 a colour ____________
12 a direction ____________

B The words that are cramped in this activity are all **opposites** to the words below. Find and write each word beside a word with an opposite meaning.

weakbentfreshbegincomeoftenrightdwarfrudeshyfatscarce

1 never ____________
2 strong ____________
3 thin ____________
4 go ____________
5 plentiful ____________
6 bold ____________
7 straight ____________
8 giant ____________
9 end ____________
10 wrong ____________
11 polite ____________
12 stale ____________

C This time the cramped words are all words that are **similar** to the ones below. Find each word and write it beside the one that has a similar meaning.

assoldtossricherrortwelvequickgiftcashfargringlad

1 wealthy ____________
2 dozen ____________
3 rapid ____________
4 present ____________
5 happy ____________
6 throw ____________
7 mistake ____________
8 donkey ____________
9 distant ____________
10 smile ____________
11 money ____________
12 aged ____________

UNIT 15A

Farm Animals

▼ **Naming Words** *(Nouns)*	ostrich swine nanny-goat heifer calf steer cattle dairy ewe bull
● **Describing Words** *(Adjectives)*	savage greedy hungry impatient gentle furry cuddly valuable protective
◆ **Action Words** *(Verbs)*	fence grunt bellow snort rear feed suckle gambol nuzzle gobble

What farm animal do you like most of all? Write a paragraph saying why you like it.

Word Meanings

Write the list words that have these meanings.

1 (▼) a large bird ______

2 (▼) a female sheep ______

3 (●) covered in fur ______

4 (●) worth a lot of money ______

5 (◆) to roar like a bull ______

6 (◆) the way a newborn baby drinks milk ______

Dictionary – What's the Word?

Add the missing letters.

1 mac _ _ _ _ _ — *pasta*

2 mag _ _ _ — *grub of a blowfly*

3 mar _ _ _ _ _ _ — *a kind of jam*

4 mat _ _ _ _ _ — *cloth*

5 matt _ _ _ _ — *base of a bed*

Word Endings – 'age'

Match each word in the box to its meaning.

language	*savage*	*village*
postage	*bandage*	*sausage*

1 small town ______

2 meat in a skin ______

3 fierce ______

4 cloth covering a wound ______

5 the words we speak ______

6 the charge to mail a letter ______

Special Words – Compound Words

Unjumble the letters in brackets on the right and add the words to the spaces on the left.

1 light ______ (ohuse)

2 life ______ (obat)

3 back ______ (ayrd)

4 egg ______ (llesh)

5 high ______ (awy)

6 foot ______ (thpa)

Word Study – People

Match each person to the item they use.

umpire	*farmer*	*policeman*
chef	*astronomer*	*doctor*

1 handcuffs ______

2 tractor ______

3 stove ______

4 stethoscope ______

5 telescope ______

6 whistle ______

Thinking

Join the word groups to make two words.

1 co/sl/ld/ow ______ ______

2 be/ar/ga/ng ______ ______

3 si/ze/fu/ll ______ ______

4 he/ro/le/af ______ ______

5 ue/tr/wh/ip ______ ______

Places and People

UNIT 15B

A Find the names of various places in the grid and write them beside the correct definition.

c	h	u	r	c	h	x
z	g	a	r	d	e	n
o	g	a	r	a	g	e
o	b	e	a	c	h	m
x	x	s	i	l	o	i
p	a	l	a	c	e	n
a	v	i	a	r	y	e
s	t	a	t	i	o	n

1 a place where cars are kept ______________________

2 a place where you can see wild animals ______________________

3 a place of worship ______________________

4 a place for swimming ______________________

5 a place where minerals are dug up ______________________

6 a place where flowers grow ______________________

7 a place where grain is stored ______________________

8 a place to catch a train ______________________

9 the home of a king ______________________

10 a place where birds are kept ______________________

B People are called different names according to their job or the role they are playing. Circle the correct word to complete each definition.

1 A (dentist pilot) cares for your teeth.

2 A very large person is a (saint giant).

3 A member of the army is a (soldier comic).

4 A member of a wandering group is a (gypsy author).

5 A soldier on guard duty is a (villain sentry).

6 One of three children born at the same time is a (twin triplet).

7 A person who saw an event is a (witness umpire).

8 One who entertains by telling jokes is a (comic captain).

9 A person renting property to another is a (landlord villain).

10 One skilled in drawing and painting is an (undertaker artist).

UNIT 16A

The Seasons

▼ **Naming Words** *(Nouns)* — storm thunder clouds raindrops barometer blizzard cyclone hues deciduous lightening

● **Describing Words** *(Adjectives)* — cold breezy chilly bleak pleasant dusty windy humid clear thundery

◆ **Action Words** *(Verbs)* — change flash growl peek fall freeze snuggle sweat burst swelter

Write two sentences explaining why you like or dislike summer, and then two explaining why you like or dislike winter.

Word Meanings

Write the list words that have these meanings.

1 (▼) a device to measure air pressure ______

2 (▼) trees that lose their leaves in winter ______

3 (●) hot with damp air ______

4 (●) light windy weather ______

5 (◆) lose moisture from the body ______

6 (◆) to change water to ice ______

Dictionary – What's the Word?

Add the missing letters.

1 mea _ _ _ _ *disease giving you spots*

2 me _ _ _ *fruit that grows on a vine*

3 me _ _ _ _ *heavenly bodies*

4 mic _ _ _ _ *germ*

5 mi _ _ _ _ *noon*

6 mi _ _ _ _ _ *error*

Word Beginnings – 'ob'

Match each word to its meaning.

1 stubborn	*obey*
2 to do as you are told	*obtain*
3 a shape	*obstacle*
4 to get something	*oboe*
5 a musical instrument	*oblong*
6 a snag; something in the way	*obstinate*

Special Words – Doubles

Add a word from the box to complete each double.

fork	*saucer*	*eggs*
moon	*blue*	*pepper*

1 black and ______

2 salt and ______

3 bacon and ______

4 cup and ______

5 knife and ______

6 sun and ______

Word Study – Syllables

Join the syllables to make a word, e.g. (ous dan ger) = dangerous.

1 (ful won der) ______

2 (bu am lance) ______

3 (ex cite ment) ______

4 (ter day yes) ______

5 (i an mal) ______

6 (vent ure ad) ______

Thinking

Add the first letter to complete each fruit.

1 __anana	2 __lum
3 __inepple	4 __each
5 __pricot	6 __pple

Add One On

UNIT 16B

In this activity you must add one letter to each word to make another word that matches the definition given. The letter may be added to any part of the word.
e.g. and *a body part* = hand

A

1	net	*bird's home*	________	2	cat	*a horse pulls one*	________
3	heat	*it pumps blood*	________	4	pin	*type of tree*	________
5	fog	*hopping creature*	________	6	stirs	*steps*	________
7	sea	*water animal*	________	8	rain	*you think with it*	________
9	sip	*large boat*	________	10	bit	*used to catch fish*	________
11	pin	*ache*	________	12	men	*unkind*	________

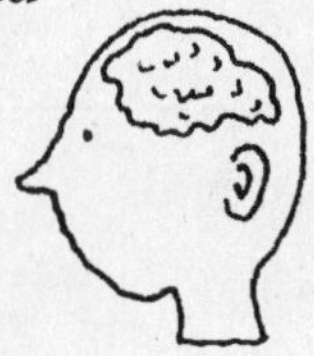

B

1	our	*sixty minutes*	________	2	cave	*to cut meat*	________
3	done	*male bee*	________	4	for	*number*	________
5	save	*cut a beard*	________	6	bother	*family member*	________
7	lower	*a rose is one*	________	8	last	*fewest*	________
9	bead	*hair on the chin*	________	10	talk	*part of a plant*	________
11	dad	*passed away*	________	12	clod	*it brings rain*	________

C

This time unjumble the letters and add a letter to make a word that matches the meaning. e.g. osn = son, *words to music* = song

1	atr	*it twinkles*	________	2	dba	*group of musicians*	________
3	acp	*type of fish*	________	4	gri	*circle*	________
5	cie	*small insects*	________	6	etn	*canvas home*	________
7	arn	*comes from the sky*	________	8	esa	*we sit on it*	________
9	asd	*grainy soil*	________	10	aml	*makes light*	________
11	oct	*clothing*	________	12	amn	*horses's hair*	________

UNIT 17A

At the Zoo

▼ **Naming Words** *(Nouns)*	nursery sanctuary aquarium enclosure cages keeper kiosk aviary trainer souvenir
● **Describing Words** *(Adjectives)*	hairy bushy savage spotted shaggy cuddly feathered sad horned gentle
◆ **Action Words** *(Verbs)*	swing chatter display breed munch exhibit scratch leap screech bite

Make a list of animals you might see at a zoo. Draw a picture of one of them.

Word Meanings

Write the list words that have these meanings.

1 (▼) a protected place for wildlife ______

2 (▼) a large cage for birds ______

3 (●) covered in feathers ______

4 (●) rough and hairy ______

5 (◆) to talk quickly ______

6 (◆) to show off ______

Dictionary – What's the Word?

Add the missing letters.

1 na _ _ _ _	*paper towel*
2 na _ _ _ _	*not wide*
3 ne _ _ _ _ _ _ _ _ _ _	*lives next door*
4 ne _ _	*bird's home*
5 ni _ _ _ _ _ _ _ _	*gas, part of the air*
6 nu _ _ _ _	*small lump of gold*

Word Endings – 'ess'

Match each word in the box to its meaning.

express	*address*	*dress*
confess	*distress*	*mattress*

1 clothing ______

2 part of a bed ______

3 where you live ______

4 trouble ______

5 not stopping ______

6 tell what you have done ______

Special Words – Anagrams

Anagrams are words made by rearranging the letters of another word.

Rearrange the letters of the words on the left to make a word that matches the definition.

1 rood	*an entance*	______
2 slot	*many*	______
3 war	*not cooked*	______
4 bare	*large animal*	______
5 deal	*heavy metal*	______

Word Study – Jumbled Letters

Unjumble the letters to make a word that matches the definition.

1 (ucrel) *very unkind* ______

2 (rcoka) *noise of a frog* ______

3 (nwocr) *a king wears one* ______

4 (nacle) *not dirty* ______

5 (efikn) *sharp tool* ______

6 (riach) *we sit on it* ______

Thinking

Add the missing letters to complete these bird names.

1 __agpie	2 __lover
3 __ren	4 __enguin
5 __agle	6 __igeon

Trucks and Cats

UNIT 17B

A Find ten words in the grid relating to **trucks.** Colour them *red.*
Find ten words in the grid relating to **cats.** Colour these *black.*

d	i	e	s	e	l	t	i	g	e	r	t
e	t	r	a	f	f	i	c	c	s	c	a
n	p	k	i	t	t	e	n	l	n	a	b
g	u	c	a	r	g	o	r	a	a	b	b
l	r	p	r	o	w	l	i	w	r	i	y
n	r	m	o	g	g	y	g	s	l	n	f
e	f	e	l	i	n	e	s	p	i	t	r
t	r	a	n	s	p	o	r	t	x	h	e
v	e	h	i	c	l	e	m	e	w	a	e
s	a	v	a	g	e	b	i	t	e	u	w
s	l	e	e	p	e	r	c	u	b	l	a
w	e	i	g	h	b	r	i	d	g	e	y

B Use a small word from the box to complete these words which are also associated with trucks.

in	*ash*	*rake*	*or*
eat	*ears*	*gin*	*net*

1 radiat______ **2** bon________ **3** b________s **4** cab__________

5 en________e **6** d______board **7** g________ **8** h__________er

C Cats are selfish animals. Do you agree?
Give reasons for your opinion.

____

____

____

____

UNIT 18A

Clothing

▼ **Naming Words** *(Nouns)*	apron belt suit sleeves sneakers jumper singlet helmet frock undies
● **Describing Words** *(Adjectives)*	warm light snuggly pretty floral comfortable tight protective untidy long
◆ **Action Words** *(Verbs)*	dress shed cuddle squeeze pull brush clean stain launder alter

Make a list of the clothes you would wear to school on a cold, rainy day. Draw pictures. Now do the same for a hot, summer's day.

Word Meanings

Write the list words that have these meanings.

1 (▼) type of footwear ____________

2 (▼) protective garment ____________

3 (●) a design with flowers ____________

4 (●) messy ____________

5 (◆) to take off clothes ____________

6 (◆) to wash and clean ____________

Dictionary – What's the Word?

Add the missing letters.

1 oa _ _ _	*fertile spot in the desert*
2 oc _ _ _	*the sea*
3 oc _ _ _ _ _ _	*eight sided shape*
4 oc _ _ _ _ _ _	*sea creature*
5 ol _ _ _	*oily fruit*
6 on _ _ _	*root vegetable*

Word Beginnings – 'dis'

Match each word to its meaning.

1 an illness	*disappear*
2 to melt like sugar in water	*discus*
3 to show off	*disaster*
4 a terrible happening	*disease*
5 a flat object that is thrown	*display*
6 to go out of sight	*dissolve*

Special Words – Homophones

Underline the correct word in the brackets.

1 Tom *(threw through)* the ball to me.

2 We hammered the *(stake steak)* into the ground.

3 Can you *(sea see)* me from there?

4 We walked *(threw through)* the thick forest.

5 The *(stake steak)* I bought from the butcher was delicious.

6 The large yacht sailed across the *(sea see)*.

Word Study – Word Groups

Colour the insect words red. Write the other words under the correct heading.

leopard	*termite*	*hare*
grasshopper	*antelope*	*plover*
sparrow	*penguin*	*wasp*

Animal	**Bird**
____________	____________
____________	____________
____________	____________

Thinking

Drop one letter to make a new word.

1 sting ________	2 four ________
3 heart ________	4 rain ________
5 send ________	6 frog ________

Two Word Cross Outs

UNIT 18B

A Each group of letters contains two words with their letters in the correct order. Find the words from the clues.

e.g. g f o l i v d e *precious metal* and *a number*
answers = **gold** and **five**

1 msotoanr *both seen in the sky at night* ______ ______

2 kpiutptpeyn *baby dog and baby cat* ______ ______

3 sbhoiapt *two things that go over water* ______ ______

4 cdoowg *two animals* ______ ______

5 gpreaapre *two fruits* ______ ______

6 zteibgrear *two animals with stripes* ______ ______

7 emaagglpeie *two birds* ______ ______

8 cbreiectkleet *two insects* ______ ______

9 pyuerlplloew *two colours* ______ ______

10 hseqxuaagroen *two shapes* ______ ______

11 gclooavte *two pieces of clothing* ______ ______

12 hteeaertth *two body parts* ______ ______

B If you cross out every second letter in the following groups you will be left with things found inside a home.

1 sxitnykp ______

2 opvteynx ______

3 czlmopczk ______

4 cdaerfpgeht ______

5 txaybzlmep ______

6 sbocfda ______

7 cfhgahinr ______

8 bpaxtdh ______

9 djovozr ______

10 kxeytxtylxey ______

11 thebldefvgihsjikoln ______

12 rzebfcrdifghejrraltmonr ______

Food

▼ **Naming Words** *(Nouns)*	pudding dessert cakes scones trifle barbeque lasagne sponge entrée soup
● **Describing Words** *(Adjectives)*	delicious tasty scrumptious tough soft horrible crunch greasy spicy creamy
◆ **Action Words** *(Verbs)*	cook boil simmer fry bake stew swallow eat steam melt

Imagine you want to prepare tea for your family because it is your mother's birthday. Write what you would cook and how you would prepare and cook it. Use at least ten of the words above.

Word Meanings

Write the list words that have these meanings.

1 (▼) type of pasta dish ____________

2 (▼) liquid food ____________

3 (●) lovely to taste ____________

4 (●) full of grease and oil ____________

5 (◆) to heat water until it bubbles ____________

6 (◆) to cook in oil ____________

Dictionary – What's the Word?

Add the missing letters.

1 pa __ __ __ __	*king's home*
2 pa __ __ __	*flower*
3 pa __ __ __ __ __	*large cat*
4 pa __ __ __ __	*colourful bird*
5 pa __ __ __ __ __ __ __	*person travelling in a moving vehicle*
6 pa __ __ __	*sticky substance*

Word Endings – 'ing'

Match each word to a link word below.

cling	*cunning*	*morning*
sting	*ring*	*string*

1 afternoon ____________

2 rope ____________

3 sly ____________

4 circle ____________

5 clutch ____________

6 bite ____________

Special Words – Synonyms

If the words mean the same put a tick in the box. If they do not mean the same put a cross in the box.

1 difficult	❑	hard	2 toss	❑	throw
3 table	❑	old	4 peace	❑	calm
5 hide	❑	conceal	6 find	❑	lose
7 cold	❑	chilly	8 heal	❑	cure
9 rob	❑	steal	10 need	❑	require

Word Study – Confused Words

Circle the correct word.

1 Sally put on her *(cloths clothes)*.

2 The boys *(writ wrote)* the answers down.

3 I wanted to *(borrow lend)* a pen from Sally.

4 We played the record *(loud loudly)*.

5 Everyone *(brought bought)* their bikes to school.

6 I think *(it's its)* time to leave.

Thinking

After each word write whether you would find it in the kitchen **(k)** or bedroom **(b)**.

1 cutlery ___	2 mattress ___
3 wardrobe ___	4 hotplate ___
5 oven ___	6 pillows ___

Our Alphabet

UNIT 19B

Our alphabet is made up of twenty-six letters arranged in alphabetical order.

A Write the *two* letters in each word that follow each other in the alphabet.
e.g. **ab**acus = ab : fir**st** = st

1 about ______ 2 toast ______
3 effigy ______ 4 reader ______
5 leopard ______ 6 ghost ______
7 himself ______ 8 kleptomaniac ______
9 notice ______ 10 drooping ______

B This time find the *three* letters side by side in each word that are in alphabetical order.

1 defence ________ 2 hijinks ________
3 dabchick ________ 4 ghilgai ________
5 calmness ________ 6 monopoly ________
7 first ________ 8 stupidly ________
9 Tuvala ________ 10 redefine ________

C Arrange each set of words below in alphabetical order to make sentences.

last	*Horace*	*Joe's*	*Monday*	*inspected*	*knee*

____

____

Friday	*every*	*brings*	*Alma*	*donuts*	*cream*

____

____

Takeaway Food

▼ **Naming Words** *(Nouns)* — hamburger pizza hot dog souvlaki pies fish and chips chicken-nuggets ice-cream sandwich dim sims

● **Describing Words** *(Adjectives)* — fried boiled baked delicious fatty greasy unhealthy soft sugary munchy

◆ **Action Words** *(Verbs)* — bite chew drink slurp spill gobble dip devour taste take

What is your favourite takeaway food? Why? Describe how you would make the 'perfect' hamburger.

Word Meanings

Write the list words that have these meanings.

1 (▼) a sausage in a bread roll ____________

2 (▼) a frozen food ____________

3 (●) cooked in oil ____________

4 (●) full of sweetener ____________

5 (◆) to grind up with the teeth ____________

6 (◆) to put into liquid ____________

Dictionary – What's the Word?

Add the missing letters.

1 pe _ _ _ *part of a flower*

2 ph _ _ _ _ _ _ _ _ _ _ *picture taken with a camera*

3 pi _ _ _ *musical instrument*

4 pi _ _ _ _ *bird*

5 pi _ _ _ _ *sea robber*

6 po _ _ _ _ _ _ _ *sea creature like a dolphin*

Word Beginnings – 'com'

Match each word to its meaning.

1 a funny program	*comb*
2 it gives directions	*comet*
3 a punctuation mark	*comic*
4 we brush our hair with it	*comma*
5 a heavenly body	*compass*
6 a picture magazine	*comedy*

Special Words – Opposites

Unjumble the letters in brackets to make a word ***opposite*** *in meaning.*

1 *early* (tlae) ____________

2 *succeed* (afil) ____________

3 *difficult* (aesy) ____________

4 *follow* (ldae) ____________

5 *gentle* (urogh) ____________

6 *question* (enaswr) ____________

7 *hairy* (abld) ____________

Word Study – Jumbled Letters

Unjumble the letters to make a word that fits the definition.

1 (roni) *metal* ____________

2 (tsfa) *very quick* ____________

3 (yopn) *small horse* ____________

4 (gede) *side of something* ____________

5 (stae) *direction* ____________

Thinking

Write ***Dead*** or ***Alive*** after each of these words.

1 divan ________	2 monkey ________
3 table ________	4 moss ________
5 duck ________	6 train ________

Sports and Weather

UNIT 20B

A Find ten words in the grid that relate to **sport**. Colour them *brown*.
Find ten words in the grid that relate to **weather**. Colour them *blue*.

u	m	p	i	r	e	c	l	o	u	d	s
l	h	g	o	a	l	s	h	o	r	t	s
i	a	a	t	r	a	i	n	b	o	w	r
g	i	t	h	r	g	a	m	e	s	w	a
h	l	h	u	e	s	l	e	e	t	h	i
t	s	l	n	f	s	h	o	e	s	i	n
n	t	e	d	e	b	a	l	l	s	s	c
i	o	t	e	r	f	i	e	l	d	t	o
n	n	i	r	e	w	i	n	d	y	l	a
g	e	c	x	e	s	u	n	n	y	e	t
x	s	s	b	a	r	o	m	e	t	e	r
a	t	m	o	s	p	h	e	r	e	x	x

B Add a small word from the box to complete the name of each sport.

box	*rick*	*foot*	*able*	*key*	*arch*

1 c_______et **2** _______ery **3** _______ball

4 hoc_______ **5** _______ing **6** t_______tennis

C Write a sentence stating your favourite season. Explain why.

____

____

____

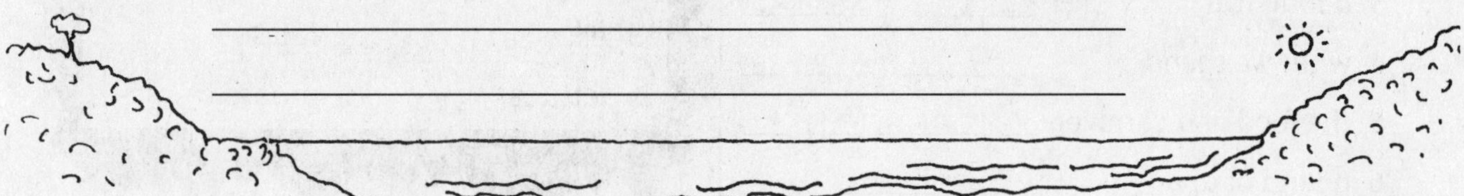

UNIT 21A

Insects and Spiders

▼ **Naming Words** *(Nouns)* — redback funnelweb blowfly eggs lice cockroach grasshopper mosquito caterpillar butterfly

● **Describing Words** *(Adjectives)* — tiny colourful venomous ugly horrible dirty crawling disease-spreading useful creepy

◆ **Action Words** *(Verbs)* — bite sting fly burrow kill spread buzz suck devour build

Write down some things that are bad about insects and spiders then write down some good things.

Word Meanings

Write the list words that have these meanings.

1 (▼) the grub of a moth ____________

2 (▼) a small insect that moves by hopping ____________

3 (●) poisonous ____________

4 (●) not clean ____________

5 (◆) to erect ____________

6 (◆) to dig into ____________

Dictionary – What's the Word?

Add the missing letters.

1 qu _ _ _ — *noise of a duck*

2 qu _ _ _ _ _ — *one fourth*

3 qu _ _ _ — *wife of a king*

4 qu _ _ _ _ _ _ _ — *opposite to answer*

5 qu _ _ _ — *without sound or noise*

Word Endings – 'ey'

Match each word in the box to its meaning.

prey	*money*	*journey*
grey	*monkey*	*honey*

1 a sweet substance ____________

2 a colour ____________

3 a long trip ____________

4 what we spend ____________

5 the food of a carnivore ____________

6 a kind of ape ____________

Special Words – Compounds

Add a word from the box to complete the word in the sentence.

roads	*prints*	*ball*
fruit	*light*	*way*

1 I play foot______ after school.

2 The policeman took his finger__________.

3 The cars collided at the cross__________.

4 There are a lot of cars on the free__________.

5 We used a flash__________ to see in the dark.

6 I like to drink the juice of a grape__________.

Word Study – Matching Words

Match each word in the box to a word below.

doctor	*cheese*	*plate*
cereal	*apricot*	*pedal*

1 saucer __________ 2 milk __________

3 bicycle __________ 4 jam __________

5 hospital __________ 6 silo __________

Thinking

After each word write ***Animal*** (A) or ***Vegetable*** (V).

1 turnip _____ 2 coyote _____

3 elk _____ 4 radish _____

5 lettuce _____ 6 moose _____

Missing Letters

UNIT 21B

A The first *two* letters of these words are missing. Add them to make a word that fits the definition.

1 __ __ able *horse's home*

2 __ __ eese *food made from milk*

3 __ __ ipping *jumping with rope*

4 __ __ idge *span over water*

5 __ __ nter *cold season*

6 __ __ emist *person who sells medicines*

7 __ __ eakfast *first meal of the day*

8 __ __ ream *to yell loudly*

9 __ __ anket *bed covering*

10 __ __ own *colour*

B The first *three* letters of these words are missing. Add them to make a word that fits the definition.

1 __ __ __ ool *place of learning*

2 __ __ __ tty *opposite to ugly*

3 __ __ __ ra *striped horse*

4 __ __ __ umn *season*

5 __ __ __ ey *bees make it for us*

6 __ __ __ icot *fruit*

7 __ __ __ nt *huge person*

8 __ __ __ usand *large number*

9 __ __ __ ar *sweetener*

10 __ __ __ ine *motor*

C Now add one letter at the beginning and one letter at the end to complete these words.

1 __irt__ *opposite of clean*

2 __row__ *a king wears it*

3 __abbi__ *small, furry animal*

4 __al__ *baby cow*

5 __ppl__ *fruit*

6 __eetl__ *insect*

7 __keleto__ *bones of the body*

8 __stronau__ *space traveller*

9 __ettuc__ *green, leafy vegetable*

10 __ans__ *flower*

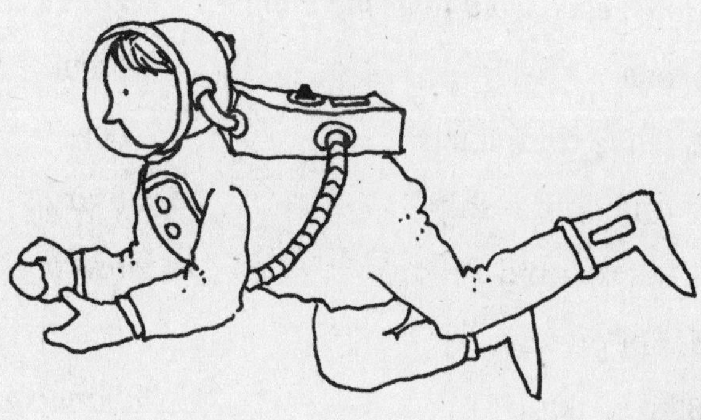

UNIT 22A

On the Move

▼ **Naming Words** *(Nouns)* — train truck transport hang-glider carriage sulky bus coach mountain-bike tricycle

● **Describing Words** *(Adjectives)* — fumy light heavy express busy crowded long-distance powerful speedy sleepy

◆ **Action Words** *(Verbs)* — speed stop grind gallop glide sail roar fly zoom reverse

What is the longest trip you have ever made? Describe it.

Word Meanings

Write the list words that have these meanings.

1 (▼) a vehicle pulled by a locomotive ______________

2 (▼) a three wheeled vehicle ______________

3 (●) very strong ______________

4 (●) not stopping ______________

5 (◆) to run like a horse ______________

6 (◆) to move across water using wind for power ______________

Dictionary – What's the Word?

Add the missing letters.

1 ra _ _ _ _ *small, furry creature*

2 ra _ _ _ _ *dried grape*

3 ra _ _ _ *sharp blade*

4 re _ _ _ _ *ingredients to make a cake*

5 re_ _ _ _ _ _ _ *person in charge of a game*

6 re _ _ _ _ _ _ _ *animal with antlers*

Word Beginnings – 'ab'

Match each word to its meaning.

1 over	*absent*
2 leave completely	*above*
3 on board a ship	*absurd*
4 silly, stupid	*absorb*
5 not present	*aboard*
6 to soak up	*abandon*

Special Words – Doubles

Add a word from the box to complete the doubles.

cream	*butter*	*lemons*
there	*round*	*square*

1 The jam contains oranges and ____________.

2 I ate some bread and ____________.

3 We had peaches and ____________ for dessert.

4 I beat him fair and ____________.

5 We ran round and ____________.

6 I searched here and ____________ for the ring.

Word Study – Rhyming Words

Circle the two words in each row that rhyme.

1	horse	hose	sauce	shore
2	halt	salt	belt	bolt
3	fairy	early	curly	barley
4	meat	dead	feet	boot
5	spider	wider	glitter	wander
6	kilt	built	flames	grand

Thinking

They were bought at a supermarket. Their names are written backwards. What are they?

1 paos ________	2 aet ________
3 tlas ________	4 klim ________
5 rettub ________	6 ragus ________

Space and Farmyards

UNIT 22B

A Ten words in the grid relate to **space.** Colour them *blue.*
Ten words in the grid relate to the **farmyard**. Colour them *yellow.*

f	c	o	m	e	t	s	w	h	e	a	t
e	s	b	h	a	s	m	a	n	u	r	e
n	t	e	a	s	p	c	m	t	p	t	h
c	a	e	r	t	a	e	e	w	l	e	a
e	r	h	v	r	c	r	t	i	a	l	y
s	s	i	e	o	e	e	e	n	n	e	s
d	p	v	s	n	s	a	o	k	e	s	t
a	l	e	t	a	h	l	r	l	t	c	a
l	o	s	m	u	i	s	x	e	x	o	c
r	u	d	o	t	p	b	a	r	n	p	k
y	g	o	o	x	o	r	b	i	t	e	x
x	h	g	n	t	r	a	c	t	o	r	x

B Add letters from the box to complete the names of farmyard animals and birds. Draw a picture of each one.

key	*or*	*at*	*it*	*owl*	*rich*	*am*	*don*

1 h____se

2 tur_____

3 go______

4 ll_____a

5 rabb_____

6 ost________

7 ______key

8 f________

Our Bodies

▼ **Naming Words** *(Nouns)*	wrist chin head toes ankle elbow neck hair tongue shoulder
● **Describing Words** *(Adjectives)*	tall short thin fat healthy bony chubby muscular handsome wrinkled
◆ **Action Words** *(Verbs)*	breathe climb pant leap stomp whack dance play kneel skip

Make a list of 5 things about your body that makes you different from your best friend.

Word Meanings

Write the list words that have these meanings.

1 (▼) the joint of your leg and foot ____________

2 (▼) the taste organ ____________

3 (●) very strong ____________

4 (●) good to look at ____________

5 (◆) to inhale and exhale air ____________

6 (◆) to lean down on one knee ____________

Dictionary – What's the Word?

Add the missing letters.

1 sa _ _ _ _	*riding seat on a horse*
2 sa _ _ _ _	*shoe with straps*
3 sar _ _ _ _	*small fish*
4 sau _ _ _ _	*meat in skins*
5 sc _ _ _ _ _ _ _	*cutting implements*
6 sh _ _ _ _ _ _	*hair soap*

Word Endings – 'or'

Match each word to its link word below.

author	*tractor*	*error*
motor	*mirror*	*razor*

1 mistake ____________

2 shave ____________

3 farm ____________

4 looking glass ____________

5 book ____________

6 engine ____________

Special Words – Anagrams

Change the order of the letters in each word in the box to make a word that matches the picture.

blow	*reap*	*hoes*	*grin*

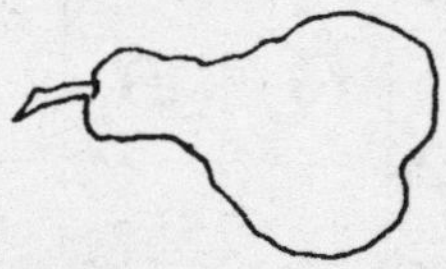

1 ____________

2 ____________

3 ____________

4 ____________

Word Study – Contractions

Write the two words that make up each contraction, e.g. it's = it is.

1 we're ________ ________

2 shouldn't ________ ________

3 couldn't ________ ________

4 I've ________ ________

5 she'll ________ ________

Thinking

Make a list of all the clothes we wear. Draw pictures of some of the things on your list.

Double Up

UNIT 23B

A Add a pair of double letters to make words that match the drawings.

 1 pu_____y	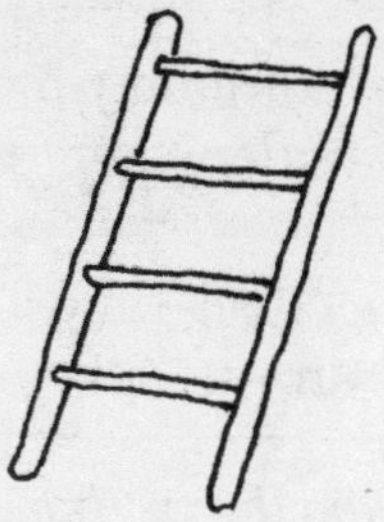 2 la_____er	 3 ke_____el
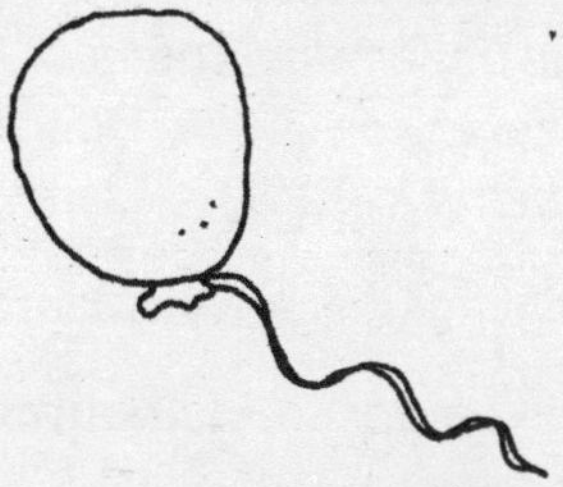 4 ba_____oon	 5 mi_____or	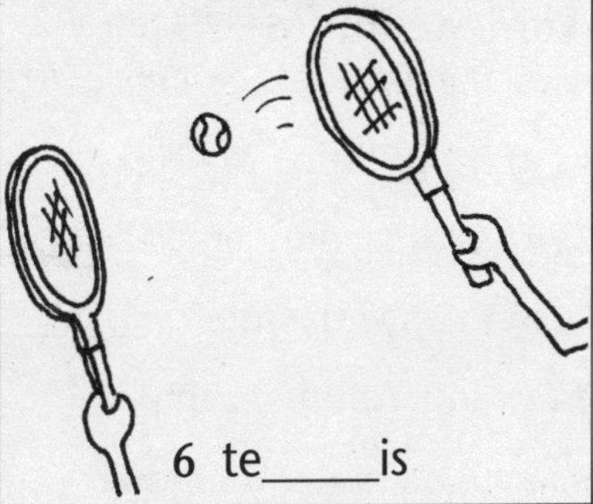 6 te_____is
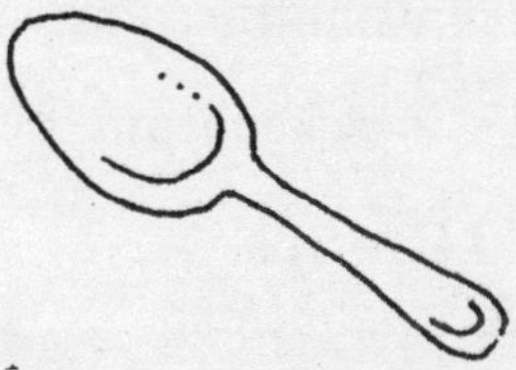 7 sp_____n	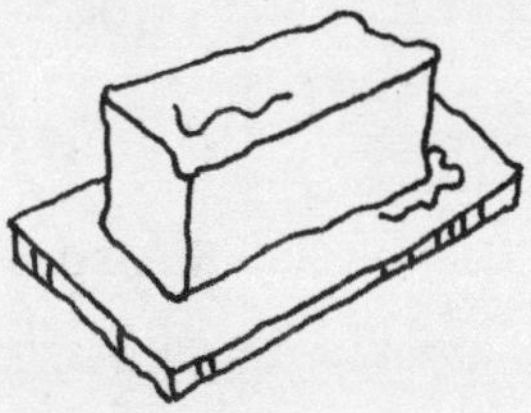 8 bu_____er	 9 gira_____e

B Find the words in the grid that have double consonants and write them beside their meanings.

p	i	z	z	a	b	e	e
s	p	a	r	r	o	w	n
b	l	o	s	s	o	m	e
t	r	a	f	f	i	c	t
p	i	l	l	o	w	x	t
w	e	d	d	i	n	g	l
c	a	b	b	a	g	e	e

1 small bird _______________

2 stinging plant _______________

3 vehicles on a road _______________

4 leafy, green vegetable _______________

5 take-away food _______________

6 an insect _______________

7 marriage _______________

8 flowers of a tree _______________

9 headrest on a bed _______________

UNIT 24A

The Ocean

▼ **Naming Words** *(Nouns)*	shark coast waves tide cuttlefish seaweed surf tsunami current breakers
● **Describing Words** *(Adjectives)*	frothy pounding gloomy deep dangerous foamy briny underwater powerful marine
◆ **Action Words** *(Verbs)*	smash crash drag dive ride rise fall surge drown boil

Make a list of some of the things that live in the ocean.
Draw pictures of them.

Word Meanings

Write the list words that have these meanings.

1 (▼) a very large wave ____________

2 (▼) a large, dangerous fish ____________

3 (●) to do with water ____________

4 (●) dull, uninteresting ____________

5 (◆) to go under the water____________

6 (◆) to die by being under water

____

Dictionary – What's the Word?

Add the missing letters.

1 ta _ _ _ _ _	*baby frog*
2 ta _ _ _ _	*picture on the skin*
3 tel _ _ _ _ _ _ _	*instrument for viewing distant objects*
4 ten _ _ _	*sport played on a court*
5 ten _ _ _ _ _	*arm of an octopus*
6 te _ _ _ _ _	*small dog*

Word Beginnings – 're'

Match each word to its meaning.

1 to mend	*release*
2 to be sorry for something you did	*ready*
3 to let go	*recipe*
4 how to make a cake	*referee*
5 prepared	*regret*
6 person in charge of a sporting match	*repair*

Special Words – Homophones

Write a word from the box in the sentences.

road	*bury*	*saw*
rode	*berry*	*sore*

1 Mike has a nasty ________ on his leg.

2 This ____________ leads to Melbourne.

3 The cowboy ________ his horse into town.

4 The dog tried to __________ the bone.

5 We _______ three birds in the cage.

6 I ate the __________ I picked from the bush.

Word Study – Word Groups

Circle the word that does not belong.

1	ship	boat	canvas	canoe
2	land	clouds	ground	earth
3	small	tiny	great	little
4	sea	ocean	milk	lake
5	hair	comb	brush	shoe
6	glue	gum	paste	scissors

Thinking

Add the missing **e** or **ee**.

1 scrch	*yell loudly*	____________
2 yar	*twelve months*	____________
3 fiv	*number*	____________
4 bll	*we ring it*	____________
5 dntist	*cares for teeth*	____________

One Letter

UNIT 24B

A Place the same letter in front of every word in the group to make a new word each time.

Example:	are		care
	at	Add the letter **c** =	cat
	age		cage

1 loud __________
art __________
row __________

2 any __________
other __________
eat __________

3 here __________
ant __________
heat __________

4 ear __________
rain __________
art __________

5 ray __________
luck __________
inch __________

6 rail __________
light __________
an __________

B Place the same *two* letters in front of every word or letter piece in the group to make a new word each time.

dr	*fl*	*br*
pr	*pl*	*cr*

1 awl __________
ink __________
other __________

2 ower __________
oat __________
own __________

3 ill __________
own __________
awn __________

4 oak __________
eek __________
awl __________

5 ease __________
aster __________
astic __________

6 owl __________
awn __________
each __________

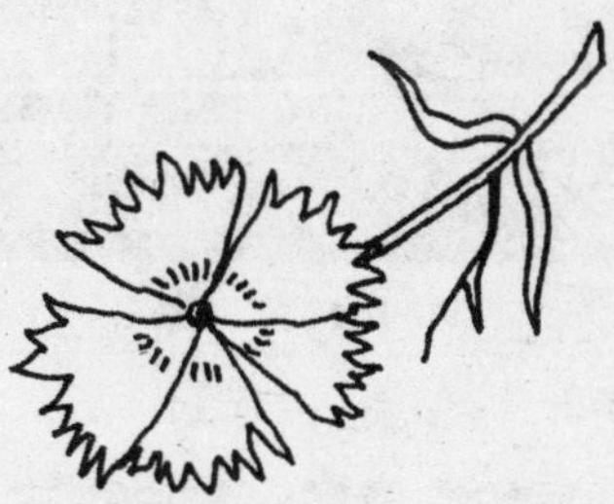

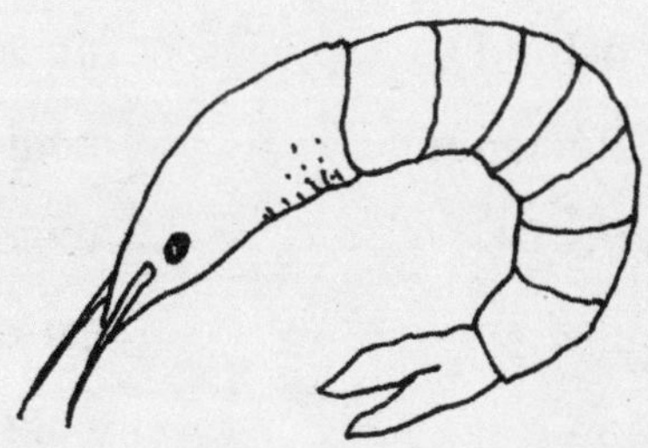

Aeroplanes

▼ **Naming Words** *(Nouns)*	airport wings jet cockpit pilot cabin tail controls fuselage hangar
● **Describing Words** *(Adjectives)*	sleek shiny large speedy supersonic comfortable crowded noisy acrobatic rapid
◆ **Action Words** *(Verbs)*	fly dive ascend glide plunge taxi take-off stall soar spin

Draw a picture of an airport. Label at least ten different things.

Word Meanings

Write the list words that have these meanings.

1 (▼) a person who flies a plane ________

2 (▼) where planes are kept ________

3 (●) very big ________

4 (●) very quick ________

5 (◆) to go up ________

6 (◆) to dive towards the earth ________

Dictionary – What's the Word?

Add the missing letters.

1 t _ _ _	*hire car*
2 t _ _ _ _	*large, striped cat*
3 to _ _ _ _ _ _ _	*day after today*
4 to _ _ _	*tall building*
5 th _ _ _	*prickle*
6 th _ _ _	*front part of the neck*

Word Endings – 'ain'

Match each word ito its meaning.

1 ache	*captain*
2 to stay behind	*mountain*
3 leader of a team	*again*
4 to be sure	*remain*
5 high hill	*certain*
6 once more	*pain*

Special Words – Synonyms

Replace each of the underlined words with one of similar meaning from the box.

middle	*false*	*smart*
boast	*speak*	*cunning*

1 Mike is a very clever ________ boy.

2 We know that it is untrue ________.

3 A fox is a sly ________ animal.

4 I ran to the centre ________ of the room.

5 She wanted to talk ________ to me.

6 Don't brag ________ about yourself.

Word Study – Similies

Add a word from the box to complete each simile.

feather	*ghost*	*pancake*
silk	*sky*	*rock*

1 as flat as a ________

2 as white as a ________

3 as light as a ________

4 as hard as a ________

5 as blue as the ________

6 as smooth as ________

Thinking

Add a set of double letters to complete each word.

1 be____	*it rings*	2 c____l	*not hot*
3 pi____	*tablet*	4 so____er	*a sport*

Alphabet Antics

UNIT 25B

A Left Out Letters

Letters have been left out of each row. Rearrange them to make a word that means the same as the one at the end of the row. The first one has been done for you.

1	__bc__efghijkl__no__qrstuvwxyz	*wet*	damp
2	__bcd__fghijk__mno__qrstuvwxyz	*jump*	
3	a__cd__f__h__jklm__opqrstuvwxyz	*start*	
4	__b__defg__ijklmnopqrs__uvwxyz	*talk*	
5	__bcd__fghijklm__opqrs__uvwxyz	*tidy*	
6	abc__ __fgh__jklmnopqrstuv__xyz	*broad*	
7	abcdefg__ijklmn__pqr__ __ __vwxyz	*yell*	
8	abcd__fghijklmn__pq__ __ __uvwxyz	*shop*	
9	__b__d__fghijklmnopq__ __tuvwxyz	*frighten*	
10	abcd__fgh__jkl__no__q__s__uvwxyz	*allow*	

B Placing Words

Circle the word that is not in alphabetical order.

For example: apple banana (grape) fig lime

1	copy	dirty	fist	happy	glad
2	help	jam	ice	kitten	lily
3	queue	mice	nine	onion	piece
4	rat	tiny	sun	uncle	velvet
5	grey	horse	ink	kennel	jam
6	apple	cat	bear	dog	ear
7	told	use	vase	xylophone	wash
8	mice	police	zebra	race	track
9	gold	joke	horse	kitten	lazy
10	cold	desert	egg	fruit	ape
11	onion	queen	salt	race	truck
12	coffee	ball	driver	horse	mouse

In the Backyard

▼ **Naming Words** *(Nouns)*	cubbyhouse patio lawn fence garden kennel rockery manure nest barbeque
● **Describing Words** *(Adjectives)*	bushy colourful messy native open shady shrubby lush large fragrant
◆ **Action Words** *(Verbs)*	build hide chase climb harvest slide throw investigate explore prune

Design your own cubbyhouse. Write down all the crazy things you would have to make it comfortable, e.g. ice-cream maker.

Word Meanings

Write the list words that have these meanings.

1 (▼) dog's home ____________

2 (▼) a grassed area ____________

3 (●) full of shrubs ____________

4 (●) sweet smelling ____________

5 (◆) to gather food ____________

6 (◆) to cut off branches ____________

Dictionary – What's the Word?

Add the missing letters.

1 um _ _ _ _ _ _	*a cover from the rain*
2 u _ _ _ _	*your mother's brother*
3 uni _ _ _ _ _	*the world, heavens etc*
4 un _ _ _ _ _	*to dig up*
5 u _ _ _	*not nice to look at*
6 und _ _ _ _	*clothing worn under other clothes*

Word Beginnings – 'em'

Match each word to its meaning.

1 hot coal	*emerald*
2 to hire a worker	*empty*
3 to leave your country to live elsewhere	*emu*
4 precious stone	*ember*
5 containing nothing	*emigrate*
6 large bird	*employ*

Special Words – Opposites

If the pairs have an opposite meaning tick the box. If they do not have an opposite meaning cross the box.

1 less	❑ more	2 right	❑ left
3 pencil	❑ crayon	4 there	❑ here
5 past	❑ future	6 fresh	❑ stale
7 speak	❑ talk	8 lead	❑ follow

Word Study – Collections

Use a word from the box to fill the spaces.

set	*swarm*	*litter*
suite	*team*	*pack*

1 a ____________ of kittens

2 a ____________ of bees

3 a ____________ of tools

4 a ____________ of cards

5 a ____________ of footballers

6 a ____________ of furniture

Thinking

Add one of the sets of double letters to complete each word. Use each set twice.

bb tt ll

1 ru____er	2 ye____ow
3 bu____er	4 ba____oon
5 blu____er	6 ba____le

Parties and Volcanoes

A Twelve words in the grid relate to **parties**. Colour them *blue*.
Eleven words in the grid relate to **volcanoes.** Colour them *red*.

c	a	k	e	c	r	a	t	e	r	p	e
j	c	o	n	e	g	a	s	e	s	r	r
e	s	t	r	e	a	m	e	r	a	e	u
l	d	e	s	s	e	r	t	x	s	s	p
l	m	o	u	n	t	a	i	n	h	e	t
y	c	o	r	d	i	a	l	s	l	n	l
b	i	r	t	h	d	a	y	i	o	t	o
r	u	m	b	l	e	x	v	n	l	f	n
e	x	p	l	o	d	e	e	g	l	e	l
m	o	l	t	e	n	x	n	x	i	a	a
s	w	e	e	t	s	x	t	x	e	s	v
a	v	a	l	a	n	c	h	e	s	t	a

B Below are actions you may **see** at a party and some you may **hear** at a party. Colour action words *yellow* and sound words *green*.

ring	drink	whoopee	giggle	gorge
sizzle	crack	eat	frolic	pop
kiss	devour	chuckle	clink	dance
click	cheer	trick	play	chatter

UNIT 27A

Balloons

▼ **Naming Words** *(Nouns)* — birthday magician tricks streamers party rubber helium clown colours presents

● **Describing Words** *(Adjectives)* — bulky colourful full-blown light stretchy tight bloated immense rubbery soft

◆ **Action Words** *(Verbs)* — burst blow inflate deflate expand float roll propel explode stretch

Make up a story about the day you floated into space holding onto balloons. Use at least 10 of the words above.

Word Meanings

Write the list words that have these meanings.

1 (▼) long strips of coloured paper ____________

2 (▼) gifts ____________

3 (●) full of colour ____________

4 (●) very large ____________

5 (◆) to grow larger ____________

6 (◆) blow up like a bomb ____________

Dictionary – What's the Word?

Add the missing letters.

1 vac _ _ _ _ _ *holiday*

2 vel _ _ _ *soft cloth*

3 va _ _ _ _ *land between hills*

4 van _ _ _ _ *flavouring*

5 va _ _ *container for flowers*

6 ve _ _ _ _ _ _ _ *carrot, onion etc.*

Word Endings – 'ant'

Match each word to its meaning.

1 very nice	*servant*
2 huge person	*vacant*
3 baby	*giant*
4 dried grape	*currant*
5 slave or helper	*infant*
6 empty	*pleasant*

Special Words – Compounds

Unjumble the letters in the brackets to make a word that, when added to the space, makes a compound word.

1 The man robbed the bee________ *(ihves).*

2 There is a large rain______ *(bwo)* in the sky.

3 I have a lot of home_______ *(owrk).*

4 Ned Kelly was an out_______ *(lwa).*

5 This watch is water________ *(ooprf).*

6 Sally has a painful tooth________ *(cahe).*

Word Study – Syllables

Join the syllables to make a word.

1 (on lem ade) ____________

2 (e tel phone) ____________

3 (ber No vem) ____________

4 (en ope vel) ____________

5 (to mos qui) ____________

6 (ine sub mar) ____________

Thinking

Add one of the letter groups to complete each word. Use each group twice.

ai ue ou

1 cl____d	2 gl____
3 st____n	4 tr____n
5 c____ld	6 bl____

Yes or No?

UNIT 27B

Answer **yes** or **no** to each question.
You may need to use a dictionary.

	Question	Yes	No
1	Has a locust got six legs?		
2	Does a guitar have strings?		
3	Could you travel across water in a dinghy?		
4	Is a ruby red?		
5	Is a sycamore a type of fish?		
6	Is a quince a type of spider?		
7	Could you eat nougat?		
8	Does a macaw have feathers?		
9	Do you get stone at a quarry?		
10	Is water stored in a silo?		
11	Is beer made at a brewery?		
12	Does a mongoose have fur?		
13	Do you blow an ukelele to make music?		
14	If you have amnesia can you remember things?		
15	Does you heart pump blood?		
16	Does the word vacation mean a holiday?		
17	Is a male horse a mare?		
18	Is a baby goose called a gosling?		
19	Is a funnelweb dangerous?		
20	Is your mothers' mother your uncle?		
21	Would you find your tongue in your mouth?		
22	Is an omelet made from eggs?		
23	If you squander money are you saving it?		
24	Would you wear a bonnet on your feet?		
25	Does a eucalypt have leaves?		

UNIT 28A

Bears

▼ **Naming Words** *(Nouns)* bamboo panda paws claws den cub forest Winnie the Pooh honey cave

● **Describing Words** *(Adjectives)* broad dangerous grizzly hairy cuddly carnivorous drowsy playful shaggy massive

◆ **Action Words** *(Verbs)* hibernate charge chase lumber prowl roll yawn strike hunt sniff

Write a story saying why your teddy bear is so special.
Draw a picture of it.

Word Meanings

Write the list words that have these meanings.

1 (▼) home of a bear ________

2 (▼) a tall grass ________

3 (●) meat eating ________

4 (●) very large ________

5 (◆) to sleep through winter ________

6 (◆) to smell ________

Dictionary – What's the Word?

Add the missing letters.

1 vill _ _ _ *small town*

2 vio _ _ _ *stringed musical instrument*

3 vio _ _ _ *flower*

4 vol _ _ _ _ _ *exploding mountain*

5 voy _ _ _ *long trip*

6 vul _ _ _ _ _ *bird of prey*

Word Beginnings – 'ad'

Match each word to its meaning.

1 to promote a product	*adopt*
2 to tell the truth	*address*
3 to move forward	*adult*
4 a grown up	*advance*
5 where you live	*admit*
6 to take as one's own	*advertise*

Special Words – Phrases

Match each word to its phrase below.

tear	*there*	*heels*
grey	*easy*	*tongs*

1 head over ________

2 here and ________

3 wear and ________

4 hammer and ________

5 free and ________

6 old and ________

Word Study – Usage

Circle the correct word.

1 We *(ain't aren't)* leaving just yet.

2 I asked her for her *(advise advice)*.

3 I want you to be very *(quiet quite)*.

4 Tom had to *(teach learn)* his brother to swim.

5 We *(told asked)* if we could borrow the bike.

6 *(May Can)* we eat the lollies?

Thinking

Make as many words as you can by using the letters in the box. Each word must contain the letter **e**.

h	a	g
a	e	d
g	t	n

Pairing Off

UNIT 28B

Write a pair of letters to make a word to match the definition.
The first one has been done for you.

A Six-letter Words

1	m	o	n	k	e	y	*an ape*
2	f	i			e	r	*a digit of the hand*
3	p	i			o	w	*we sleep on it*
4	c	h			c	h	*a place to pray in*
5	d	o			o	r	*a person who cares for the sick*
6	c	a			l	e	*cows, bulls, calves*
7	e	n			n	e	*motor*
8	l	a			e	r	*climbing steps*
9	p	i			i	c	*an outdoor meal*
10	b	u			e	t	*a missile fired from a gun*
11	a	n			e	r	*opposite to a question*
12	v	o			g	e	*a long trip in a ship*

B Seven-letter Words

1	c	a			a	g	e	*leafy, green vegetable*
2	q	u			t	e	r	*one fourth*
3	c	e			u	r	y	*one hundred years*
4	w	h			t	l	e	*an umpire blows it*
5	c	h			n	e	y	*it lets smoke out*
6	b	l			s	o	m	*flowers of a tree*
7	v	i			t	o	r	*caller*
8	d	e			e	r	t	*sweets after a meal*
9	m	i			i	o	n	*large number*
10	r	o			t	e	r	*male fowl*
11	d	i			a	s	e	*illness*
12	l	i			a	r	y	*place for reading books*

Bicycles

▼	**Naming Words** *(Nouns)*	axle frame chain reflector tube seat helmet tyre spokes brake
●	**Describing Words** *(Adjectives)*	broken speedy rickety modern rusty sturdy shiny flat mangled shaky
◆	**Action Words** *(Verbs)*	brake coast glide pedal shake bump skid steer whiz accelerate

Design and draw your own supersonic bicycle. Label the parts. Use at least five words from above.

Word Meanings

Write the list words that have these meanings.

1 (▼) a hard hat ____________

2 (▼) the rubber inside part of a tyre ____________

3 (●) new, up to date ____________

4 (●) strong ____________

5 (◆) to stop ____________

6 (◆) to speed up ____________

Dictionary – What's the Word?

Add the missing letters.

1 wa _ _ _	*middle of your body*
2 wall _ _ _	*animal like a kangaroo*
3 w _ _ _	*stinging insect*
4 we _ _ _ _ _ _	*rich*
5 we _ _ _	*strange*
6 wh _ _ _	*largest of all creatures*

Word Endings – 'dle'

Match each word to its meaning.

1 the centre of a circle	*needle*
2 riding seat on a horse	*paddle*
3 a kind of dog	*saddle*
4 a wax tube with a wick	*poodle*
5 an oar for a canoe	*middle*
6 a sewing implement	*candle*

Special Words – Anagrams

Find and write the pairs of words that contain exactly the same letters. Write them in pairs.

l	w	s	v	s	a	l	t
a	o	t	e	w	e	s	t
s	l	e	i	f	l	o	w
t	f	w	l	l	i	v	e
s	a	l	e	r	i	n	y
g	r	i	n	s	e	a	l

eg. last ____ salt ____

1 ____________ ____________

2 ____________ ____________

3 ____________ ____________

4 ____________ ____________

5 ____________ ____________

Word Study – Rhyming Words

Circle the two words in each row that rhyme.

1	shower	grower	flower	lawyer
2	face	ears	tore	cheers
3	first	fist	word	worst
4	red	blue	said	hard

Thinking

Add a pair of letters to complete each word. Use each pair twice.

bl tr sw

1 ____allow	2 ____ain
3 ____ue	4 ____actor
5 ____imming	6 ____izzard

Adding Words

UNIT 29B

A Add a *small word* from the box to make each word in the grid.
The first one has been done for you.

add	*all*	*able*	*can*	*air*	*and*
ant	*age*	*ache*	*ace*	*act*	*are*

1	c	h	a	i	r			*something we sit on*
2				a	r	y		*small bird*
3	s	t						*horses home*
4	p	a	l					*home of a king and queen*
5	t	e					r	*person who helps you learn*
6	t	r				o	r	*farm machine*
7	w				e	t		*container for money*
8	s				a	l	s	*footwear with straps*
9	s	a	u	s				*meat with skins*
10				r	e	s	s	*where you live*
11	i	n	f					*baby*
12	s	q	u					*four sided shape*

B Choose the correct *small word* to complete each word.
Draw a picture of each word you make.

(ask ass)
1 gr__________

(ant and)
2 gi__________

(art ran)
3 o__________ge

(and all)
4 sw__________ow

(ask ash)
5 b__________et

(ate ass)
6 pir__________

UNIT 30A

Bulldozers

▼ **Naming Words** *(Nouns)*	blade bucket wheels engine gearstick construction site tracks Caterpillar earth gravel
● **Describing Words** *(Adjectives)*	huge hard-working smoky slow powerful gradual heavy mighty deafening violent
◆ **Action Words** *(Verbs)*	bump bulldoze demolish crumble destroy flatten pulverise vibrate steamroll crush

Make up a fun story about the day you drove a bulldozer. Write down all the things you knocked down. Use at least 10 words from the list.

Word Meanings

Write the list words that have these meanings.

1 (▼) small stones ______________

2 (▼) a motor ______________

3 (●) very strong ______________

4 (●) very, very loud ______________

5 (◆) to level out ______________

6 (◆) destroy a building ______________

Dictionary – What's the Word?

Add the missing letters.

1 wa _ _ _ _	*container for paper money*
2 wal _ _ _	*ocean animal*
3 wa _ _	*a magician's tool*
4 we _ _ _ _ _ _	*marriage*
5 wh _ _ _	*cereal*
6 wi _ _ _ _	*kind of tree*

Word Beginnings – 'inter'

Match each word to its meaning.

1 holding one's attention	*interfere*
2 meddle in other's affairs	*interesting*
3 the inside of a house	*interrupt*
4 concerning different nations	*interior*
5 where two roads meet	*international*
6 break into a conversation	*intersection*

Special Words – Homophones

Use a word from the box to fill each space.

peace	*nose*	*pale*
piece	*knows*	*pail*

1 I am sure Mike ____________ who stole it.

2 The ____________ is full of water.

3 I would like one ____________ of pie please.

4 The countries now live in ____________.

5 Sam had blood pour from his ____________.

6 Sally's skin is ____________ after her illness.

Word Study – Word Groups

Add a word from the box to complete each group.

grapefruit	*sandals*	*pillow*	*rattle*

1 shoes boots galoshes ______________

2 cot bib dummy ______________

3 lemon orange lime ______________

4 sheet blanket mattress ______________

Thinking

Add a pair of letters to complete each word. Use each pair twice.

dr	cr	fr

1 ____og	2 ____ane
3 ____ain	4 ____ust
5 ____agon	6 ____ost

Witches and Whales

A In this grid eleven words relate to **witches**. Colour them *green*. Twelve words relate to **whales** and the sea. Colour them *blue*.

b	b	r	o	o	m	s	t	i	c	k	p
l	g	p	l	a	n	k	t	o	n	e	o
u	o	m	a	g	i	c	a	l	c	v	d
b	b	w	i	c	k	e	d	x	a	i	u
b	l	d	o	l	p	h	i	n	l	l	g
e	i	h	a	r	p	o	o	n	f	m	l
r	n	s	p	e	l	l	s	f	c	a	y
w	i	z	a	r	d	x	x	l	l	m	k
b	l	o	w	h	o	l	e	o	i	m	r
p	o	r	p	o	i	s	e	a	c	a	i
b	l	a	c	k	c	a	t	t	k	l	l
c	a	u	l	d	r	o	n	f	l	y	l

B Add a letter group from the box to complete the name of each creature that lives in the ocean. Draw a picture.

ark	*to*	*ab*	*star*	*ale*

1 oc____pus   2 cr______   3 ________fish   4 sh______   5 wh______

A Funny Clown

▼ **Naming Words** *(Nouns)*: circus joker make-up busker fire-eater pantomime streamers comedian custard-pie big top

● **Describing Words** *(Adjectives)*: clever funny foolish strange slapstick wonderful zany awkward masked whimsical

◆ **Action Words** *(Verbs)*: chuckle crash giggle smash leap whoop whack squeak mimic dance

Make up a story about the clown who couldn't make people laugh. Use at least 10 list words.

Word Meanings

Write the list words that have these meanings.

1 (▼) a person who makes us laugh ______________

2 (▼) large circus tent ______________

3 (●) clumsy ______________

4 (●) amusing ______________

5 (◆) to copy ______________

6 (◆) to laugh quickly ______________

Dictionary – What's the Word?

Add the missing letters.

1 ya _ _ _ — *ship with sails*

2 ya _ _ — *when you are tired*

3 y _ _ _ — *twelve months*

4 ye _ _ _ _ — *shouted*

5 ye _ _ _ _ — *colour*

6 ye _ _ _ _ _ _ _ — *the day before today*

Word Endings – 've'

Match each word to its meaning.

1 to cut off a beard	*hive*
2 to make better	*dove*
3 something we can cook things in	*shave*
4 clothing worn on the hand	*stove*
5 a bird	*improve*
6 a bee's home	*glove*

Special Words – Synonyms

Match the words with similar meanings.

ring	*accept*	*hide*	*discover*
dozen	*hobby*	*queer*	*goblin*

1 receive ______ 2 peal ______

3 strange ______ 4 elf ______

5 conceal ______ 6 twelve ______

7 interest ______ 8 find ______

Word Study – Matching Words

Match each word in the box to a word below.

globe	*vein*	*cereal*
water	*pupil*	*fish*

1 artery ______ 2 hook ______

3 kettle ______ 4 lamp ______

5 breakfast ______ 6 eye ______

Thinking

Add a pair of letters to complete each word. Use each pair twice.

br ch fl

1 ____our 2 ____ick

3 ____eese 4 ____icken

5 ____ipper 6 ____own

Adding Words

UNIT 31B

Add a small word from the box to make a word to match the picture.

eat	*can*	*ball*	*oar*	*ice*	*imp*
even	*ear*	*owl*	*pea*	*one*	*oak*

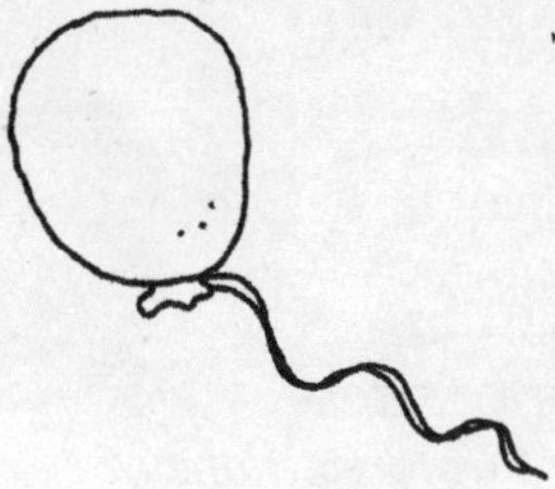 1 _______oon	 2 _______dle	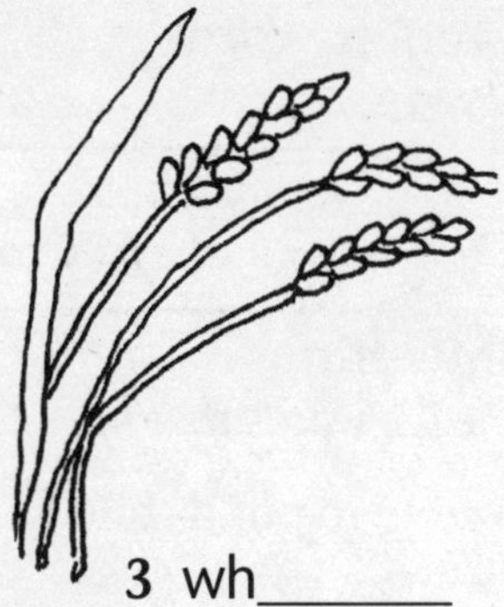 3 wh_______
 4 b_______	 5 el_______	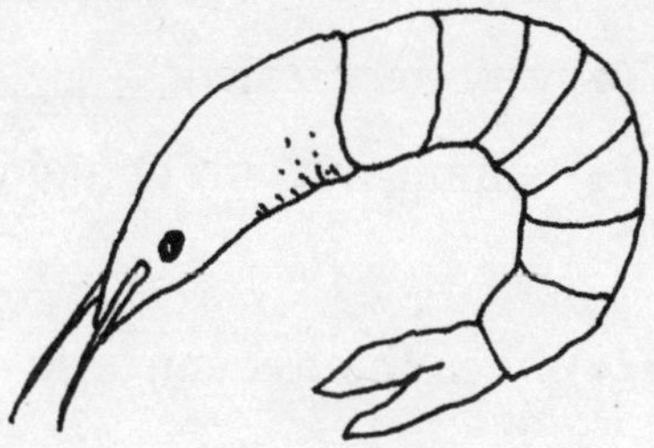 6 shr_______
 7 m _______	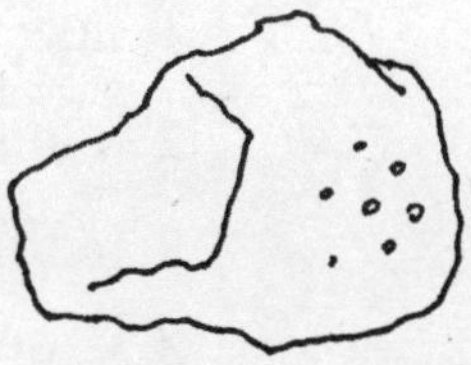 8 st_______	 9 cupb_______d
 10 cl_______	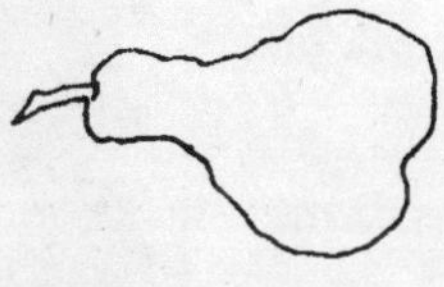 11 _______r	 12 b_______

UNIT 32A

In the Dark

▼ **Naming Words** *(Nouns)*	fear midnight nightmare sunset sunrise torch ghost sleep lullaby dawn
● **Describing Words** *(Adjectives)*	black spooky cloudy starless moonless sombre terrified nocturnal dreadful ghostly
◆ **Action Words** *(Verbs)*	collide darken frighten grope stumble scare torment tumble panic knock

Imagine you are left at home by yourself. Late at night you hear a noise in the backyard. Write what happens. Use some of the list words.

Word Meanings

Write the list words that have these meanings.

1 (▼) a song to put a child to sleep ________

2 (▼) a scary dream ________

3 (●) very, very scared ________

4 (●) coming out only at night ________

5 (◆) when things bump into each other ________

6 (◆) to feel around in the dark ________

Dictionary – What's the Word?

Add the missing letters.

1 sq _ _ _ _	*four-sided shape*
2 pe _ _ _ _	*used in a car*
3 pi _ _ _ _	*type of bird*
4 fli _ _ _ _ _	*a penguin's wings*
5 cr _ _ _ _	*drawing implement*

Word Beginnings – 'per'

Match each word to its meaning.

1 allow to do something	*periscope*
2 distance around the outside of a shape	*perfume*
3 instrument to see above water	*perch*
4 sweet smelling scent	*perfect*
5 place for birds to sit	*perimeter*
6 excellent, just right	*permit*

Special Words – Opposites

Replace the underlined word with one of opposite meaning.

light	*return*	*noisy*
succeed	*repair*	*sorry*

1 Our class is always quiet ________.

2 When will we leave ________?

3 This parcel is heavy ________.

4 I'm glad ________ he didn't come.

5 We will damage ________ the door.

6 I am sure he will fail ________.

Word Study – Definitions

Match each word to its definition.

1 not proud	*ignore*
2 a long walk	*youth*
3 to take no notice of	*humble*
4 joint of the hand	*coarse*
5 young people	*trek*
6 rough, not fine	*wrist*

Thinking

Cross out the first letter then every second one. Write the word left over.

1 mgxaptyez ________

2 tblodaztx ________

3 tcxaykbex ________

4 xstnzobwy ________

Adding Letters

UNIT 32B

Add two letters from the box to make a word to match the picture.

For example: _leph_nt + *ea* = *e*leph*a*nt.

er	*oe*	*ab*	*al*	*lo*	*ae*
ai	*ng*	*bn*	*el*	*cn*	*iw*

1 h__rs__

2 l__m__

3 b__l__

4 h__a__t

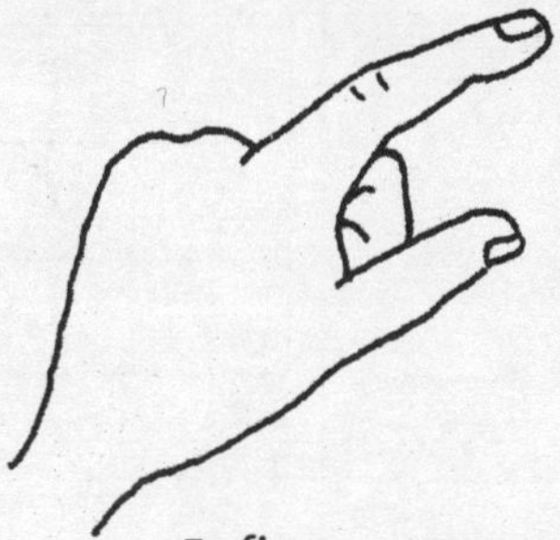

5 fi__ __er

6 r__bb__t

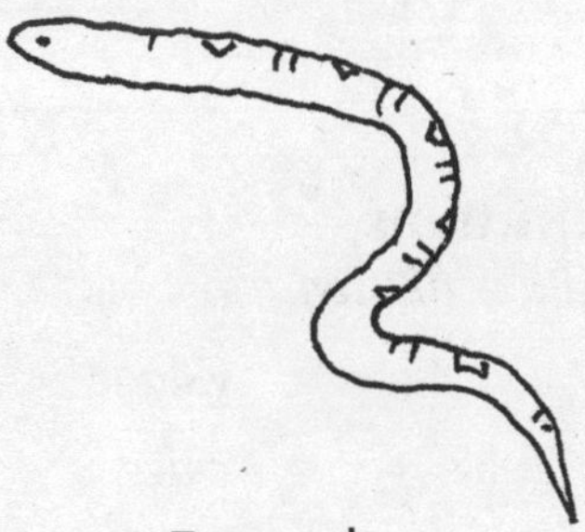

7 sn__k__

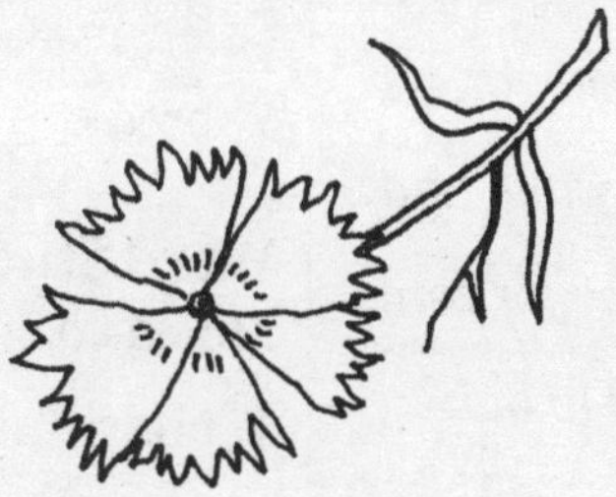

8 f__ __wer

9 w__ndo__

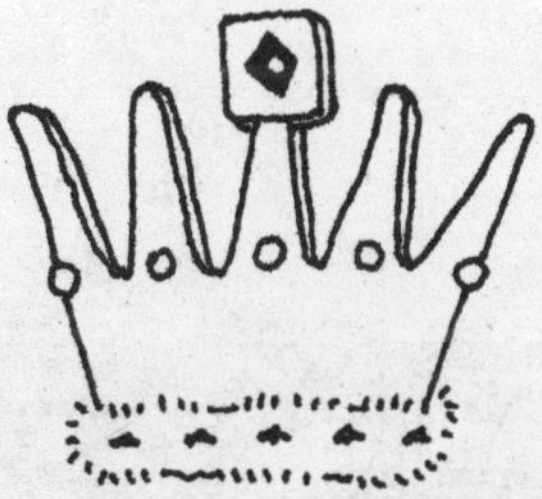

10 __row__

11 cam__ __

12 __a__ana

UNIT 33A

Elephants

▼	**Naming Words** *(Nouns)*	herd bull tusk circus mammoth Africa India ivory jumbo poachers
●	**Describing Words** *(Adjectives)*	brawny crinkly powerful wrinkled gentle clever tusked caring grey hard-working
◆	**Action Words** *(Verbs)*	trumpet squirt heave ramble sway squash strain trudge batter whack

Write a fact sheet on elephants. Write at least 5 facts. Use some of the list words.

Word Meanings

Write the list words that have these meanings.

1 (▼) people who illegally shoot elephants ____________

2 (▼) an extinct type of elephant ____________

3 (●) intelligent ____________

4 (●) having tusks ____________

5 (◆) an elephant's noise ____________

6 (◆) move from side to side ____________

Dictionary – What's the Word?

Add the missing letters.

1 ma _ _ _ _ *it attracts steel objects*

2 ma _ _ _ _ *a black and white bird*

3 mai _ _ *another name for corn*

4 mar _ _ _ _ _ _ _ *food similiar to butter*

5 mea _ _ _ _ *a disease*

6 me _ _ *list of food to eat*

Word Endings – 'ion'

Match each word to its meaning.

1 a new device *onion*

2 a place where trains stop *excursion*

3 a root vegetable *question*

4 opposite to answer *carnation*

5 a flower *station*

6 a school outing *invention*

Special Words – Compounds

In the grid find words to add to the words below. Make compound words.

p	o	r	t	x	g	m
f	b	i	r	d	r	a
l	f	i	r	e	a	r
y	f	a	s	t	p	k
f	i	e	l	d	h	x

1 air____________ 2 book____________

3 butter____________ 4 car____________

5 bush____________ 6 black____________

7 break____________ 8 photo____________

Word Study – Definitions

Match each word to its definition.

1 body fluid *village*

2 baby bear *cider*

3 apple drink *blood*

4 small town *mirror*

5 spear *cub*

6 looking glass *javelin*

Thinking

Put these words in alphabetical order to make a sentence.

dessert cold Friday every Alf buys

Football and Frogs

UNIT 33B

A Thirteen of the words in the grid relate to **football.** Colour them *orange.*
Twelve words relate to **frogs.** Colour them *green.*

g	o	a	l	s	s	p	a	w	n	k	w
c	t	o	a	d	e	g	g	s	x	i	a
r	b	a	l	l	r	e	e	d	s	c	t
o	m	a	r	k	p	o	n	d	x	k	e
a	t	a	d	p	o	l	e	x	x	e	r
k	a	m	p	h	i	b	i	a	n	d	x
t	a	c	k	l	e	b	o	u	n	c	e
s	c	r	a	m	b	l	e	h	o	p	x
s	h	i	r	t	f	r	o	n	t	x	n
i	n	s	e	c	t	s	p	l	o	p	e
d	o	d	g	e	u	m	p	i	r	e	w
b	o	u	n	d	a	r	y	p	i	e	t

B In Box 1 make a list of creatures *smaller* than a frog.
In Box 2 make a list of creatures *larger* than a frog.

1	2

UNIT 34A

Fish

▼ **Naming Words** *(Nouns)* — fillet bait net line hook sinker rod reel gills school

● **Describing Words** *(Adjectives)* — bony freckled little puffy slimy tiddly delicious striped elongated undersized

◆ **Action Words** *(Verbs)* — catch dive dodge release veer swim scatter dangle nibble jerk

Make a list of some things that live in the ocean.
Draw pictures of them.

Word Meanings

Write the list words that have these meanings.

1 (▼) a piece of boneless fish ____________

2 (▼) breathing organs of a fish ____________

3 (●) nice to eat ____________

4 (●) thin and long ____________

5 (◆) to pull suddenly ____________

6 (◆) to move about in all directions ____________

Dictionary – What's the Word?

Add the missing letters.

1 cath _ _ _ _ _ _ *large church*

2 bu _ _ _ _ _ *home of a rabbit*

3 an _ _ _ _ _ *keeps a ship in one place*

4 gl _ _ _ _ _ _ *person who eats too much*

5 fr _ _ _ _ _ _ *coloured spot on the skin*

6 ma _ _ _ _ _ *animal that feeds its young on milk*

Word Beginnings – 'en'

Match each word to its meaning.

1 to enclose in a circle	*envelope*
2 finished	*encircle*
3 container for a letter	*ended*
4 to go inside	*enemy*
5 foe	*engine*
6 motor	*enter*

Special Words – Anagrams

Rearrange the letters of the words in the box to make a word to complete the sentence.

lance	*palm*	*doer*
panel	*amble*	*please*

1 He ____________ the horse yesterday.

2 He lit the ____________ to see in the dark.

3 Mike is so tired he is still ____________.

4 Don't ____________ me for being late.

5 We must ____________ up this dirty room.

6 A jet ____________ flew overhead.

Word Study – Syllables

Put the syllables in correct order to make a word.

1 (sep ate ar) ____________

2 (ter dis as) ____________

3 (der stand un) ____________

4 (ter car pen) ____________

5 (Sep ber tem) ____________

6 (er cise ex) ____________

Thinking

Write these words that all begin with *sta.*

1 home of a horse ____________

2 a series of steps ____________

3 used to send a letter ____________

4 it twinkles at night ____________

5 to go without food ____________

Missing Letters

UNIT 34B

Add a letter to name the picture. You may need to use the letter more than once.
For example: *lphant* If we add *e* twice we can write *elephant*.
Write the full word on the line below.

A

	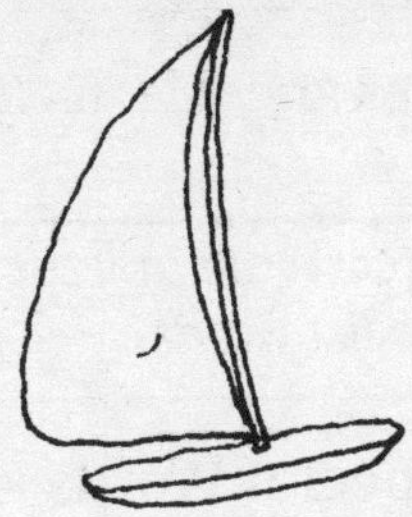		
pple	sil	cke	str
1 __________	2 __________	3 __________	4 __________

B

		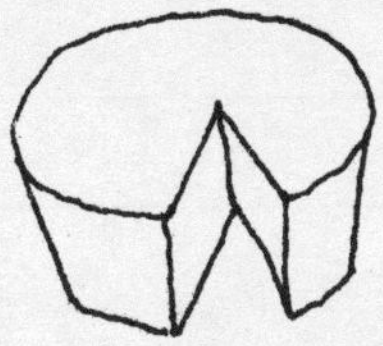	
shp	twnty	chse	kn
1 __________	2 __________	3 __________	4 __________

C

		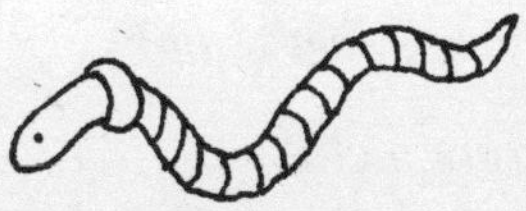	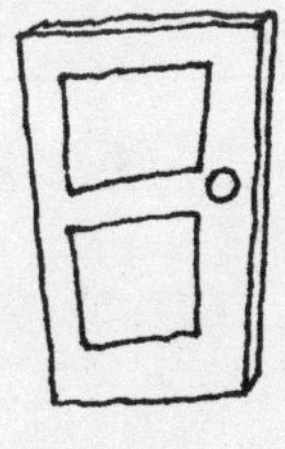
brm	flwer	wrm	dr
1 __________	2 __________	3 __________	4 __________

D

	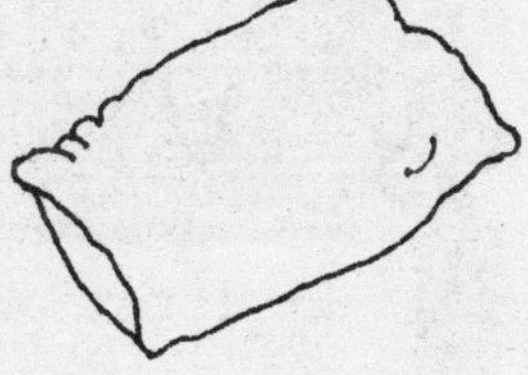	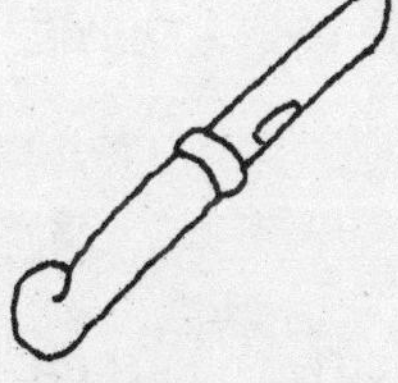	
lght	pllow	knfe	char
1 __________	2 __________	3 __________	4 __________

UNIT 35A

Cold Days

▼ **Naming Words** *(Nouns)*: frost fog dawn icicle snow rain frostbite Jack Frost jumper scarf

● **Describing Words** *(Adjectives)*: bleak chilly freezing frigid frosty icy silvery crackling wintry frozen

◆ **Action Words** *(Verbs)*: bite chatter shiver tremble melt freeze droop jump shake thaw

Write a fact sheet about winter. Write at least 5 facts. Use some of the list words.

Word Meanings

Write the list words that have these meanings.

1 (▼) thick cloud ____________

2 (▼) daybreak ____________

3 (●) turned to ice ____________

4 (●) like winter ____________

5 (◆) sag, hang down ____________

6 (◆) to shake with cold ____________

Dictionary – What's the Word?

Add the missing letters.

1 mill _ _ _ *large number*

2 stat _ _ _ _ _ _ _ *envelopes, papers etc*

3 trea _ _ _ *thick, sweet liquid*

4 z _ _ _ *white metal*

5 per _ _ _ _ _ _ _ *distance around a shape*

6 gr _ _ _ _ _ _ _ _ _ _ _ *your mother's mother*

Word Endings – 'ic'

Match each word ito its meaning.

1 used to make bottles, toys etc.	*picnic*
2 cars, buses on a road	*elastic*
3 a stretchy cord	*mechanic*
4 having to do with electricity	*traffic*
5 a meal outdoors	*plastic*
6 a person who fixes cars	*electric*

Special Words – Homographs

Use each word twice to fill the spaces.

spoke *left* *kind*

1 Mike writes with his ________ hand.

2 Sally is a very ________ helpful girl.

3 The teacher ________ to me yesterday.

4 The ________ on my bicycle wheel snapped.

5 He ________ the party early.

6 What ________ of bird is that?

Word Study – Similies

Add a word from the box to complete each simile.

nails	*ice*	*bitter*
tortoise	*lamb*	*cucumber*

1 as ____________ as a lemon

2 as gentle as a ____________

3 as hard as ____________

4 as cold as ____________

5 as cool as a ____________

6 as slow as a ____________

Thinking

Circle the two letters that follow each other in the alphabet, e.g. about = (ab)out

1 toast	2 reader
3 himself	4 baby
5 ghost	6 notice

Back to Front

UNIT 35B

The words in this grid have four letters but they are all written backwards.
Find each word and write it under the correct heading below.
Words can be across or down but none are diagonal.

n	o	i	l	a	e	l	f
n	h	t	p	b	m	a	l
a	t	a	s	r	a	e	b
w	o	o	a	e	u	l	b
s	m	g	w	k	c	u	d
f	k	l	y	k	n	i	p
l	w	a	e	d	a	e	h
a	a	o	r	n	i	k	s
c	h	f	g	k	c	e	n

Animal | **Bird** | **Insect**

Baby Animal | **Colour** | **Body**

UNIT 36A

Hot Days

▼ **Naming Words** *(Nouns)*	ashes bushfire summer oven furnace perspiration thirst shade northerly sun
● **Describing Words** *(Adjectives)*	hot humid sticky fiery sunny sweaty blazing boiling searing scorching
◆ **Action Words** *(Verbs)*	bake flare blister boil perspire smoulder scorch ignite scald stagger

Make a facts chart about summer. Write at least 5 facts.
Use some of the list words.

Word Meanings

Write the list words that have these meanings.

1 (▼) a hot season ____________

2 (▼) water coming from the body ____________

3 (●) moist, damp ____________

4 (●) reflecting heat ____________

5 (◆) heat water until it bubbles ____________

6 (◆) burst into flame ____________

Dictionary – What's the Word?

Add the missing letters.

1 gor _ _ _ _ *large ape*

2 fal _ _ _ *bird of prey*

3 cyg _ _ _ *baby swan*

4 au _ _ _ _ *season of the year*

5 cri _ _ _ _ *game*

6 car _ _ _ *floor covering*

Word Beginnings – 'im'

Match each word to its meaning.

1 to push under water	*impolite*
2 rude	*imp*
3 unable to be done	*imitate*
4 to copy	*immerse*
5 small goblin	*improve*
6 to make better	*impossible*

Special Words – Homophones

Unjumble the letters of the second word to make a homophone.

1 right *(wiret)* ____________

2 source *(usace)* ____________

3 steel *(astel)* ____________

4 would *(wdoo)* ____________

5 tow *(teo)* ____________

6 mayor *(rmae)* ____________

Word Study – Word Groups

Colour the fruit words red. Write the other words under the correct heading below.

daffodil	*pliers*	*violet*
nectarine	*carnation*	*lemon*
chisel	*lychee*	*scissors*

Tool	Flower
____________	____________
____________	____________
____________	____________

Thinking

Place the same letter in front of each word to make three new words.

e.g. _are _at _age (+c) = care cat cage

1 _ring _read _owl	2 _air _an _old
3 _tray _till _tone	4 _all _old _are
5 _at _ice _are	6 _and _ate _ass

Supermarkets and Boats

UNIT 36B

A In the grid twelve words relate to **supermarkets.** Colour them *blue.* Thirteen words relate to **boats.** Colour them *yellow.*

b	a	r	g	e	c	a	s	h	i	e	r
r	t	r	o	l	l	e	y	h	u	l	l
a	g	r	o	c	e	r	i	e	s	x	s
f	o	c	e	a	n	c	a	r	g	o	e
t	e	s	c	a	l	a	t	o	r	p	a
a	s	h	o	p	p	e	r	s	s	r	b
n	v	e	s	s	e	l	x	s	a	i	a
c	h	a	r	b	o	u	r	e	i	c	k
h	y	a	c	h	t	x	b	l	l	e	e
o	s	a	i	l	o	r	u	l	x	x	r
r	b	a	s	k	e	t	y	e	a	t	y
c	h	e	c	k	o	u	t	d	e	c	k

B Add the small words from the box to make the names of things you would be able to buy at a supermarket.

our	*rots*	*ages*	*real*	*ead*	*soa*
ants	*but*	*ham*	*ears*	*ink*	*che*

1 car______ 2 fl______ 3 ce______

4 saus______ 5 p______ 6 pl______

7 ______ter 8 s______poo 9 br______

10 dr______ 11 ______p 12 ______ese

unit contents

	1	2	3	4	5	6	7	8	9	10	11	12	13	14
Word Meanings	•	•	•	•	•	•	•	•	•	•	•	•	•	•
Dictionary	•	•	•	•	•	•	•	•	•	•	•	•	•	•
Word Endings	•		•		•		•		•		•		•	
Homophones	•					•						•		
Word Study	•	•	•	•	•	•	•	•	•	•	•	•	•	•
Matching Words		•												
Thinking	•	•	•		•		•	•	•	•	•	•	•	•
Anagrams											•			
Word Beginnings		•		•		•		•		•		•		•
Synonyms		•					•						•	
Opposites			•					•						•
Compound Words				•					•					
Contractions				•	•									
Collections					•									
Doubles/Rhymes					•					•				
Word Groups						•						•		
Syllables								•						
Confused Words			•											•
Jumbled Words														
Similes/Definitions					•									

15	16	17	18	19	20	21	22	23	24	25	26	27	28	29	30	31	32	33	34	35	36
•	•	•	•	•	•	•	•	•	•	•	•	•	•	•	•	•	•	•	•	•	•
•	•	•	•	•	•	•	•	•	•	•	•	•	•	•	•	•	•	•	•	•	•
•		•		•		•		•		•		•		•		•		•		•	
			•						•						•					•	•
•	•	•	•	•	•	•	•	•	•	•	•	•	•	•	•	•	•	•	•	•	•
•	•	•	•	•	•	•	•	•	•	•	•	•	•	•	•	•	•	•	•	•	•
		•						•						•					•		
	•		•		•		•		•		•		•		•		•		•		•
				•						•						•					
					•						•						•				
•						•					•	•			•		•				
								•													
											•										
	•						•							•			•	•	•	•	•
			•						•						•						•
	•											•							•		
				•									•								
		•			•																
										•							•	•		•	

terminology

Word Meanings
In this activity children must match or use a word from the Theme List.

Dictionary
Students must complete a word in which they are given starting letters and a defintion.

Word Endings
These are the groups of letters (suffixes) added to the end of words, e.g. teach + er = teacher.

Word Beginnings
These are the letters added to the beginning of a word to change or modify its meaning,
e.g. in + visible = invisible.

Homophones
Words which sound the same but have different meanings and different spellings,
e.g. rein : rain : reign.

Anagrams
Words that contain exactly the same letters as another but in a different order,
e.g. meat : mate : team : tame.

Synonyms
Words that have the same or similar meanings, e.g. warm : hot .

Opposites
Words that have opposite meanings, e.g. hot : cold.

Compound Words
Words made up of two or more smaller words, e.g. rain + bow = rainbow.

Contractions
Words in which a letter has been left out and an apostrophe added in its place,
e.g. do not = don't.

Collections
Words that name collections of things, e.g. a bunch of grapes.

Doubles
Words that go together, e.g. fish and chips, salt and pepper.

Rhymes
Two or more words that sound the same, e.g. gate : late : fate.

Syllables
A group of letters with one sounded vowel.
e.g. Into contains two syllables, in to.

Similes
We use similes to compare one thing to another.
e.g. He swims like a fish.